Mrs Zawade

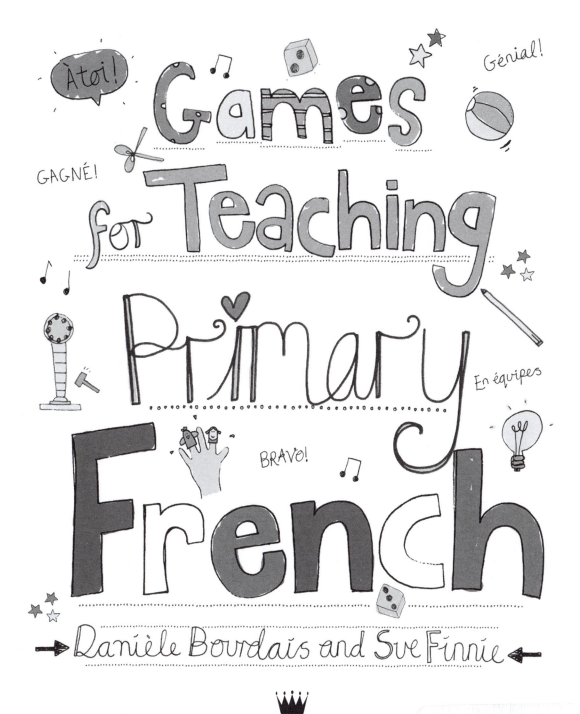

Games for Teaching Primary French

Danièle Bourdais and Sue Finnie

Crown House Publishing Limited
www.crownhouse.co.uk
www.crownhousepublishing.com

D0303390

First published by
Crown House Publishing
Crown Buildings,
Bancyfelin,
Carmarthen,
Wales, SA33 5ND, UK
www.crownhouse.co.uk

and

Crown House Publishing Company LLC
PO Box 2223, Williston, VT 05495, USA
www.crownhousepublishing.com

British Library Cataloguing-in-Publication Data
A catalogue entry for this book is available from the British Library.

Print ISBN: 978-184590-994-9
Mobi ISBN: 978-178583-033-4
ePub ISBN: 978-178583-034-1
ePDF ISBN: 978-178583-035-8

LCCN 2015952663

Printed and bound in the UK by
TJ international, Padstow, Cornwall

Contents

Introduction

Games for teaching primary French is a practical toolkit containing a wide variety of fun and engaging games for all abilities, from complete beginners to more competent learners. It includes a wide range of activities, from five-minute starters or plenaries to longer, more challenging games where learners can make substantial progress. It has been devised specifically for busy teachers with limited resources, budget and planning time, who want simple, effective ideas to use in the classroom.

Un tableau, des stylos et ce livre ... (A board, some pens and this book ...)

A board, some pens and this book will allow you to deliver outstanding, fun and engaging lessons. This book is packed with techniques and activities to support your existing scheme of work and will provide you with plenty of inspiration and ideas. The straightforward, reliable, no-tech suggestions are based on sound pedagogy and years of classroom experience, and will deliver great learning outcomes lesson after lesson.

Les jeux (The games)

Games aren't just for fun! Recent research has found that, 'In Year 6, learners seem to value learning for its own sake, [such as] games, songs, learning about cultural aspects, writing for a purpose' and recommended that 'Primary teachers should continue to include in their teaching those activities that motivate learners the most – those based on interaction, creativity, cultural contact and purposeful communication. These are most likely to promote the positive attitudes to language learning that are needed for successful learning in the secondary phase.'[1] Clearly, games are a great way to practise language while keeping motivation and engagement levels high. They can also help build pupils' confidence. What is more, research and classroom experience tell us that learners enjoy them and that they help create positive learning experiences.

Quand et comment utiliser les jeux (How and when to play)

Whatever you want to practise, you'll find a suitable game here. When to use the games is up to you. They are a great way to start or end a lesson. They make handy time-fillers or breaks in longer lessons. Put two or three games together, and you have a ready-made lesson with very little advance preparation. The book includes whole-class games, pair and group work, and individual games. There are plenty of old favourites, as well as some new, exciting ideas. You know your class best, so these games are designed for you to adapt to suit your circumstances.

---

1   Suzanne Graham, Louise Courtney, Theo Marinis and Alan Tonkyn. *Primary Modern Languages: the impact of teaching approaches on attainment and preparedness for secondary school language learning. Executive summary.* (2014). Available at: https://progressandpreparednessinprimarylanguages.files.wordpress.com/2014/06/uor-executive-summary-primary-modern-languages.pdf

You won't find games grouped by topic. The idea is that most games can be used with any topic you choose. There are noisy games and quiet games. Many are competitive, but some encourage pupils to collaborate and cooperate. Games cater for differentiation so that the winners are not always the most able pupils. Broadly speaking, the games are suitable for beginners and early learners, working at level A1 of the Common European Framework.[2] Each game can be adapted for any level but, in general, the games at the end of each part are more challenging than those at the beginning.

Think of these games as your building blocks: a set of ready-made activities that you can build into any lesson or topic. Put them together in different combinations, or adapt them to suit you!

Écouter, parler, lire et écrire (Listening, speaking, reading and writing)

The primary language classroom is an ideal space in which to practise the key competencies that are at the heart of the national curriculum – spoken language, vocabulary development and reading and writing. Learning a new language at an early age also affords pupils the chance to develop lifelong language learning skills, explore differences and similarities between languages, and make connections with other aspects of their learning. Games allow learners to absorb and explore language in a variety of mediums, building up skills, knowledge and confidence in the process.

The games in this book cover all core aspects of the primary French curriculum and are organised into the key skills areas of listening, speaking, reading and writing, with additional parts on grammar, number games and sounds. However, inevitably, different skills will be developed in combination, as learners are encouraged to listen and respond, talk and write, and so on. In Part 3: Reading, there are a number of games which link the sound, spelling and meaning of words and phrases. Songs, rhymes and drama games allow pupils to explore the patterns and sounds of the language in a fun, age-appropriate way.

To save planning time, we've tried to make all the games as user-friendly and simple to navigate as possible. For each game, you will find:

- the aims, skills and resources involved
- a step-by-step description of how to play
- useful French phrases
- variations and additional ideas
- differentiation ideas.

We hope you will find the right games for each class, and they will provide a jumping-off point for some truly engaging lessons.

Amusez-vous bien ! (Have fun!)

---

2   For more information about the Common European Framework please see http://www.coe.int/t/dg4/linguistic/cadre1_en.asp

Part 1: Listening

Listening is an important skill which should be practised as often as possible. If you play these games regularly, even for just a few minutes at a time, then pupils should soon develop confidence.

Pupils need to listen attentively to spoken language and show understanding by joining in and responding. In some of the games, all that is needed is a physical response to show that pupils have understood; in others, listening goes hand in hand with speaking.

Songs, rhymes and drama games allow pupils to explore the patterns and sounds of the language in a fun, age-appropriate way. See some suggestions on page 245.

Many of the games in Part 2: Speaking also involve listening practice, and Part 3: Reading contains a number of games that link the sound, spelling and meaning of words and phrases.

1 Four corners/*Les quatre coins*

Step by step

1. Introduce four new words. For example: *un chien/un chat/un lapin/une tortue* (a dog/a cat/a rabbit/a tortoise). Hold up each flashcard in turn, saying what it represents. Repeat each word or phrase twice, e.g. (showing picture of dog): *Un chien. ... Un chien.*

2. Ask pupils to invent a mime for each one, for example moving their arm like a wagging tail, or panting, for a dog. Then show the cards again, naming each one in turn, and let pupils do the matching mime.

3. Pin a flashcard in each corner of the room, naming it as you do.

4. When you call out a word, pupils point to the corresponding corner. Anyone who is wrong is out, and watches the rest of the class to spot any pupils who make a mistake.

Classroom management	Whole class
Skill	Listening
Aim	To present new vocabulary
Resources	Flashcards to represent the vocabulary you want to teach Adhesive tack or drawing pins

 Useful phrases

Écoutez et inventez un mime. Listen and invent a mime.
Montrez la bonne image. Point to the right picture.

Comments

- If you can play the game in a large hall, pupils can all run to the corner with the flashcard that corresponds to the word you call out. This makes it more obvious if anyone is wrong!

- To vary the activity, show a flashcard and ask a question, which pupils must answer with *oui* or *non*. For example:

  Teacher (T): *C'est une tortue ?* (Is it a tortoise?)

  Pupil (P): *Oui/Non.*

 Increase the level of challenge by calling out the names more quickly, or by including the word in a sentence, e.g. *Tu as un chat à la maison ?* (Have you got a cat at home?) or *Qui aime les lapins ?* (Who likes rabbits?)

2   Silly me!/*Étourdi !*

Step by step

1. Choose three or four pupils to stand at the front, facing the class. Give each a different flashcard or object to hold and show the rest of the class. If you are teaching colours, the objects could be socks of different colours, for instance.

2. Introduce the puppet or soft toy to the class. Pupils greet the puppet. Explain that he doesn't understand French very well so they need to help him.

Classroom management	Whole class
Skill	Listening
Aim	To revise key language
Resources	A hand puppet or soft toy Flashcards or objects representing the language to be practised

3. Make a statement practising the language you want to revise.

   For example:

   T: *Bleu !* (Blue) or *Ma couleur préférée, c'est le bleu* (My favourite colour is blue).

4. Move the puppet forward to one of the objects/flashcards. If he goes to the correct one, pupils must clap their hands and call out: *Oui, bravo !* (Yes, well done!). If he goes to the wrong object/flashcard, pupils must shake their heads and say: *Non, ce n'est pas ça !* (No, it's not that one!).

   The puppet need not always be wrong, but will generally need a couple of tries before getting it right.

5. Once you have done this a few times, a pupil can take over working the puppet.

Useful phrases

Voici <name of puppet>.	This is <name of puppet>.
Bonjour, <name of puppet>.	Hello, <name of puppet>.
C'est bien ?	Is that right?

Comments

- Make sure all pupils can clearly see the cards or objects being held up at the front of the class.
- Build up a bit of suspense as you move the puppet towards a card or object. He may move to an object slowly or change his mind at the last minute.
- For speaking practice, pupil volunteers can take over, saying the words or phrases that the puppet has to react to.

Increase the challenge by asking pupils to memorise the order of the cards or objects. Then the pupils at the front turn their backs to the class, concealing their card or object. Once the puppet has made his choice and the class has decided if it is correct or not, the pupils at the front can all turn round to see whether the puppet *and* the class were right or wrong.

Increase the level of linguistic challenge by having more pupils/flashcards and objects at the front. That way, a lucky guess is more unlikely. We suggest using up to eight pupils at a time.

Notes

....

....

....

....

....

....

....

....

....

....

....

....

....

....

....

3 Dog and bone/*L'os et les chiens*

Step by step

1. Play this game in a hall or outdoors. Divide the class into two teams. The pupils are the 'dogs' who want to get the 'bone'. The teams stand in two lines facing each other, with a large gap for running between the teams.

Classroom management	Whole class
Skill	Listening
Aim	To revise vocabulary
Resources	Soft object, e.g. soft toy, scarf or beanbag

2. Give each child a word from the vocabulary set you want to revise.
   For example, if you are revising months of the year: A: *janvier*, B: *février*, C: *mars*, D: *avril*, E: *mai*, F: *juin*, G: *juillet*, H: *août*, I: *septembre*, J: *octobre*, K: *novembre*, L: *décembre*.
   Both teams have the same words, but not in the same order (i.e. pupils with the same word should not be immediately opposite each other). For example, Team B might have: A: *mars*, B: *septembre*, C: *janvier*, D: *juin*, etc.

3. Put a soft object such as a soft toy, a beanbag or a scarf on the floor in the middle between the teams. This is the 'bone'.

4. Call out a word or sentence containing the word. For example:
   T: *Avril!* (April) or *Mon anniversaire est en avril* (My birthday is in April).

5. The pupil from each team who has that word runs forward to pick up the object in the centre before her opposite number. Whoever grabs it first wins a point for their team.

Useful phrases

Mettez-vous en rang.	Line up.
Vous êtes les chiens.	You are the dogs.
Attrapez l'os.	Grab the bone.

Comments

* This is a traditional playground game in France, where it is called *Le béret*. Traditionally, the object placed in the centre was a beret, often worn by schoolboys up to the mid-twentieth century.

To increase the level of challenge, add this rule (from the game of *Le béret*): once a dog has got the bone, they can be stopped by the other dog if she manages to touch him. The bone must then be put back in the middle.

Notes

....

....

....

....

....

....

....

....

....

....

....

....

....

....

....

....

....

....

4 Catch the ball!/*Attrape !*

Step by step

1. Play this game in a hall or play-ground. Pupils stand in a large circle.
2. Go round the circle telling each pupil their unique word. For example, if you have been learning about food and drink, you might say:
   T: *Tyler ... les chips* (crisps), *Emma ... le fromage* (cheese), *Josh ... la glace* (ice cream), etc.

Classroom management	Whole class
Skill	Listening (and speaking)
Aim	To revise key vocabulary words
Resources	A soft ball or beanbag

3. Stand in the centre of the circle. As you call out a word, throw the ball in the air.
4. The pupil who has that word moves to the centre to catch the ball.
5. If the catch is successful, the catcher throws the ball back to you, repeating the word.
6. Any pupil who drops the ball is out, and sits on the floor. The winner is the last pupil in the game.

Useful phrases

Écoutez bien votre mot.   Listen carefully to your word.

Si je dis votre mot, attrapez le balle.   If I say your word, you catch the ball.

Comments

- Try to make sure everyone gets at least one go.
- To add a speaking element, you could ask pupils to react when you are giving out the words. For example, for items of food or drink they could say whether or not they like it:

   T: *Le poulet.*

   P: *Super, j'adore le poulet* (Great, I love chicken).

   T: *Le hamburger.*

   P: *Ah non, je n'aime pas les hamburgers* (Oh no, I don't like burgers).

   Pupils could keep count to see if there are more positive than negative responses.

Increase the level of challenge by using the words in a sentence. For example,

T: *Je voudrais du pain* (I'd like some bread).

À midi, je mange du riz (For lunch, I eat rice).

Ma mère n'aime pas les tomates (My mum doesn't like tomatoes), etc.

Notes

....

....

....

....

....

....

....

....

....

....

....

....

....

....

....

....

....

....

5 Simon says/*Jacques a dit*

Step by step

This traditional game is well suited to language practice.

Classroom management	Whole class
Skill	Listening
Aim	To listen and respond physically (pupils do not need to speak)
Resources	None

1. You are the leader and stand in front of the class. If the group is small enough, you stand with pupils in a circle.

2. You give instructions, naming a part of the body pupils must touch.

   For example:

   T: *Touchez-vous les pieds/les genoux/la tête/les oreilles/le nez/la bouche/les épaules* (Touch your feet/knees/head/ears/nose/mouth/shoulders).

   Pupils only obey the instruction if it begins with the words *Jacques a dit*.

   T: *Jacques a dit: Touchez-vous les pieds* (Simon says, Touch your feet).

   Class: all touch their feet.

   If you do not start the instruction with the words *Jacques a dit*, for example, you say: *Touchez-vous les oreilles*, pupils must not obey. They stay still. You might need to give each instruction twice.

3. When someone follows an order that does not start with *Jacques a dit*, he is out of the game. Pupils who are out can still be actively involved. They come to the front and spot if anyone is making a mistake.

4. Repeat the instructions until only one pupil is left.

Useful phrases

Écoutez et faites comme moi.	Listen and do what I do.
Perdu !	You're out!
Je n'ai pas dit « Jacques a dit ».	I didn't say 'Simon says'.

Comments

- The example above practises parts of the body. You could play the same game with verbs of movement, sports or hobbies, with pupils miming the actions.

  For example: (verbs of movement) *Jacques a dit: Sautez !* (jump), *dansez !* (dance), *marchez !* (walk), etc.

(sports) *Jacques a dit: Je joue au foot* (I play football), *Je fais de la natation* (I swim), *Je joue au tennis* (I play tennis), etc.

(hobbies) *Jacques a dit: Jouez aux jeux électroniques* (play video games), *dessinez!* (draw), etc.

- When the game is familiar, pupils can play in small groups, with an able pupil taking on the role of the leader.

 Increase the challenge by increasing the speed at which you call out the instructions.

Notes

....

....

....

....

....

....

....

....

....

....

....

....

....

....

6 Line bingo/*Loto en ligne*

Step by step

This is a variation of traditional bingo.

1. Give each pupil a strip of paper. Dictate (or let them copy from the board) the words or phrases you want them to revise. They choose eight and write them in any order down their long strip of paper.

    For example, for weather vocabulary, they might write:

Classroom management	Whole class
Skill	Listening (writing and reading)
Aim	To revise known vocabulary or phrases
Resources	Sheets of A4 paper, cut vertically to make three strips. You will need one strip per pupil

2. You act as the caller. Call each word or phrase twice (you may want to check that pupils have located the correct word or phrase). They listen out for just *two* of the words or phrases on their list, the one at the top and the one at the bottom. If their word/phrase is called, they tear it off. The next word along is now at the top or bottom and becomes one of the words to listen out for when the game continues.

3. Pupils' lists get gradually shorter as they tear off the phrases they hear. You can call each phrase several times, as necessary.

4. The winner is the first player with no words or phrases left. She can call: *J'ai gagné !* (I've won!)

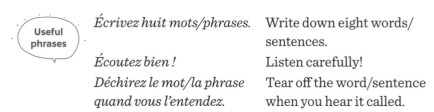

Useful phrases	*Écrivez huit mots/phrases.*	Write down eight words/sentences.
	Écoutez bien !	Listen carefully!
	Déchirez le mot/la phrase quand vous l'entendez.	Tear off the word/sentence when you hear it called.

Comments

*   If you prefer, pupils could draw symbols to represent the different types of weather instead of copying down the phrases.
*   Once they are familiar with the game, pupils can play again in small groups, with a pupil acting as caller.
*   Pass round a waste-paper bin at the end to collect all the discarded words.

Make the game more linguistically challenging by including the words or phrases in a short text, e.g. *Ce matin, je ne joue pas au football parce qu'il pleut et je n'aime pas jouer dehors quand il fait froid*. (This morning, I'm not playing football because it's raining and I don't like to play outside when it's cold.)

Notes

....

....

....

....

....

....

....

....

....

....

....

....

....

....

....

....

....

....

....

7   Stand up, sit down/*Assis, debout*

Step by step

1. Call out a statement, practising the language you want to revise. For example, if you have been teaching descriptions of people, you might say:

   T: *Josie a les cheveux courts* (Josie has short hair).

   Lauren est grande/petite (Lauren is tall/short).

   Matthew est blond/brun/roux (Matthew has blond/brown/red hair).

   Stacey a les cheveux raides/frisés (Stacey has straight/curly hair).

   Ben porte des lunettes (Ben's wearing glasses), etc.

Classroom management	Whole class
Skill	Listening
Aim	To practise listening and responding to known phrases
Resources	None

2. If the statement is true, pupils stand up. If it is false, they stay seated. Anyone who is wrong is out, and comes to the front to spot others who slip up.

3. The game continues until only one person is left.

4. A confident pupil could take over your role and call out the true/false statements.

Si c'est vrai, mettez-vous debout.	If it's true, stand up.
Si c'est faux, restez assis.	If it's false, stay sitting.
Écoutez et regardez vos camarades.	Listen and watch your classmates.

Comments

- If pupils are slow to be caught out, you could adapt the game so that the last person to react is out. This discourages pupils from waiting to see how the majority react before they move.

- A similar elimination game would be to ask all pupils to stand and then get different groups to sit down, e.g.

   T: *Assieds-toi si tu as les yeux bleus/les cheveux longs*, etc. (Sit down if you have blue eyes/long hair, etc.).

You could progress to a similar activity where pupils have to speak, rather than just give a physical response (see Liar on page 44).

8 Mastermime!/*À vos mimes !*

Step by step

1. Play this game in the hall or playground. Divide the class into two teams. Pupils spread out so they have space around them.

Classroom management	Whole class
Skill	Listening
Aim	To revise vocabulary
Resources	None

2. Make a series of statements containing an action verb or phrase. Pupils mime the action. For example, if you are practising the language for daily routine, you might say:

   T: *Je me brosse les dents* (I brush my teeth).

   Je me lave (I have a wash).

   Je m'habille (I get dressed).

   Je mange des céréales (I eat some cereal).

   Je bois du lait (I drink some milk).

   Je fais mes devoirs (I do my homework), etc.

3. Pupils who do the wrong mime are out, and watch out for others who are wrong.

4. The winner is the last pupil standing.

Useful phrases

Écoutez et mimez les actions.	Listen and mime the actions.
C'est le mauvais mime !	It's the wrong mime!
Tu as perdu !	You've lost!

Comments

- If pupils are not making mistakes and it is hard to catch them out, you could switch to eliminating the slowest child to react.

If you have a mixed class, you could make the game a bit harder by making statements that only refer to girls OR boys.

For example:

T: *Les filles se lavent* (The girls have a wash): only girls do the mime.

Les garçons s'habillent (The boys get dressed): only the boys do this.

9   True or false?/*Vrai ou faux ?*

Step by step

Classroom management	Whole class
Skill	Listening
Aim	To revise vocabulary
Resources	Two chairs, two A4 sheets with the words '*VRAI*' and '*FAUX*' Adhesive tack

1. Fix an A4 sheet with the word '*VRAI*' (true) in bold letters to the back of one chair, and '*FAUX*' (false) to the other.

2. Divide the class into two teams. Each team stands in a line facing the chairs, which are placed at the front, one behind the other, but with some space between them.

3. Make a statement practising the language you want to revise. The two pupils at the head of the line race to sit on the correct chair to win a point. For example, if you have been learning about special holidays, you might say:

   La Saint-Valentin est en février (St Valentine's Day is in February).

   As the statement is true, the pupils at the top of the line race to sit on the '*VRAI*' chair. The winner scores a point for his team.

4. Those two pupils then move to the back of the line.

5. Make a new statement and the pupils who are at the front compete to be first onto the correct chair.

6. The game continues until all pupils have had a go. Add up the points to find the winning team.

Écoutez bien la phrase.	Listen carefully to the sentence.
Si c'est vrai, asseyez-vous ici.	If it's true, you sit here.
Si c'est faux, asseyez-vous là.	If it's false, you sit there.

Comments

• The game is best played in a hall or large open space.

Here is an alternative true/false game you can play without having pupils move around. It allows you to make more challenging sentences for more able pupils, while still catering for the rest.

Divide the class into teams of three or four pupils. The teams take turns to ask you for a statement. They must choose either a one-, two- or three-point statement. The statements increase in difficulty.

For example:

T: *Pour un point: Noël est en décembre* (Christmas is in December).

Pour deux points: On fête Noël en hiver (We celebrate Christmas in winter).

Pour trois points: Le Père Noël apporte des œufs en chocolat (Father Christmas brings chocolate eggs).

Notes

....

....

....

....

....

....

....

....

....

....

....

....

....

10 Prediction/*Le devin*

Step by step

Classroom management	Whole class
Skill	Listening (and writing and speaking)
Aim	To consolidate vocabulary
Resources	None

1. In English, explain to pupils that in this game they have to try to predict something about you. Depending on the topic you want to revise, this could be, for example, your favourite clothes, sports, animals, vegetables, ice cream flavours, etc. You could write five items in order of preference on a piece of paper before the class begins and keep it in your pocket.

2. Pupils write on a piece of paper three items they predict will be your favourites. For example, for animals, they might write (or they could draw pictures) *les lions* (lions), *les chevaux* (horses), *les singes* (monkeys).

3. You read out your top five and pupils listen. They score one point if they have predicted your number 5, two points for number 4, three points for number 3, four points for number 2 and the maximum five points if they have correctly predicted your number 1 choice. If the topic is animals, you might say, for example:

   T: *Voici la liste de mes animaux préférés* (Here's the list of my favourite animals).

   Numéro cinq, c'est les éléphants (Number 5, elephants).

   Numéro quatre, c'est les vaches (Number 4, cows).

   Numéro trois, c'est les tigres (Number 3, tigers).

   Numéro deux, c'est les chiens (Number 2, dogs).

   Et numéro un, c'est ... c'est ... les chevaux ! (And number 1 is ... is ... horses!)

4. Pupils add up their scores and the one with the most points is the winner.

Useful phrases	*Devinez (mes animaux préférés).* — Guess (my favourite animals).
	Écrivez trois prédictions. — Write three predictions.
	Écoutez mon top cinq. — Listen to my top five.

Comments

- To support pupils who might find coming up with or writing the predictions a challenge, you could write ten or twenty names on the board in random order for them to choose three from.

- To add a speaking element, ask pupils to feed back their scores in French (*zéro point* for those who did not score). You could also play again, with pupils predicting the favourites of one of the more able pupils, who then tells the class her top five.

To make the game a bit harder, pupils could make four or five predictions.

Give your top ten instead of your top five if you want pupils to listen for longer.

Notes

....

....

....

....

....

....

....

....

....

....

....

....

....

....

....

....

....

11 Beep/*Bip bip*

Step by step

1. Read out a sentence or short paragraph with a key word replaced with the word « *bip bip* » or, if you have one to hand, a squeak from a squeaky toy or a buzz from a buzzer.

   For example, if you have been learning the names of shops, you could say:

   T: *Ce matin, à la boulangerie, j'ai acheté une « bip bip »* (This morning, at the baker's I bought a *beep*).

   Answer: *baguette* (French loaf).

   J'adore les fruits, alors je vais acheter des pommes et des « bip bip » (I love fruit so I'm going to buy some apples and some *beep*).

   Answer: *bananes* (bananas).

   On vend des timbres à la « bip bip » (They sell stamps at the *beep*).

   Answer: *poste* (post office).

2. Pupils suggest what the missing word might be. Acknowledge all sensible guesses until someone comes up with the right answer.

3. Make this a class v. teacher game by awarding a point to the class if they guess the missing word in under five goes. If they don't guess correctly by then, you score a point.

Classroom management	Whole class (or small groups)
Skill	Listening (and speaking)
Aim	To practise listening to continuous speech to identify missing words
Resources	Optional: squeaky toy, buzzer or similar

Useful phrases

C'est quoi, le bip bip ?	What's the beep word?
Non, ce n'est pas ça.	No, it's not that.
Oui, c'est possible, mais je pense à autre chose.	Yes, that's possible, but I'm thinking of something else.
Bravo, c'est ça !	Well done, that's it!

Comments

- The 'beep' word should always be a word that pupils are familiar with. If they are having real trouble guessing it, you could write the first and last letters of the word on the board as a clue.
- Once you have played the game as a whole class, pupils could play in small groups.

Increase the level of challenge by using an extract from a familiar story, poem or song rather than a random sentence.

Notes

....

....

....

....

....

....

....

....

....

....

....

....

....

....

....

....

....

....

....

12 Changing chairs/*Changez de chaise*

Step by step

Classroom management	Whole class
Skill	Listening
Aim	To listen for specific information
Resources	Chairs (one fewer than there are pupils) A text (using the language you are focusing on) and a list of questions Optional: audio equipment if available

1. Before the lesson, prepare a text with language you want to practise and comprehension questions based on it. If you have access to audio equipment, you could use a recording.

2. Play the game in a hall or outdoors, with plenty of space for pupils to move around. Arrange the chairs as for a game of musical chairs.

3. Tell pupils a little about what they are going to hear, e.g. a French child is going to talk about what she does at the weekend. Then set your class a question, in English or in French, depending on the level of the class, e.g. Where does Lola have her breakfast?

4. Pupils walk around the chairs as you play the recording or read the text aloud. When they hear the answer to the question, they sit on one of the chairs.

5. Pause the recording/your reading and ask the seated pupil to give you the answer to your question. (If more than one pupil is seated, ask each in turn to whisper the answer in your ear.) If the answer is correct, the pupil remains seated. If the answer is wrong, the pupil stands up again.

6. Ask another question based on what you know the pupils will hear next in the recording.

7. All pupils still standing walk round the chairs again until they hear the answer. The game continues as above. Keep asking questions and giving pupils the chance to win a seat. For the final question, only two pupils will compete for a single chair.

Useful phrases

Écoutez la question. Listen to the question.

Asseyez-vous quand vous entendez la réponse. Sit down when you hear the answer.

Comments

- If you are using a recording, keep a copy of the script to refer to when asking/answering questions.

- If you do not have a long recording or text, use several short ones, one after the other.

Make the game more difficult by asking more challenging questions.

Notes

....

....

....

....

....

....

....

....

....

....

....

....

....

....

....

....

....

13 The right order/*Le bon ordre*

Step by step

1. Prepare your story before the lesson. This could be a traditional story like Little Red Riding Hood, or you could make up a short narrative.

2. Either make a set of small cards to illustrate key words or phrases for each pupil or pair, or ask pupils to draw the pictures to make their own mini-cards. If you are working on the topic of sports and hobbies, you might make five cards with pictures of, for example, a TV, musical notes and a pair of headphones, a football, a piano, a bike.

    To go with those cards, you could use a simple text like this:

    Lundi, Jojo regarde la télé. Bof! Il n'aime pas ça. (On Monday, Jojo watches TV. It is nothing special. He doesn't like TV.)

Classroom management	Whole class
Skill	Listening
Aim	To revise vocabulary and identify individual words within a longer speech
Resources	A story or short paragraph containing the words or phrases you want to practise A set of small picture cards for each pupil or pair, representing the key words or phrases from your text (or paper or blank card for pupils to make their own flashcards)

Mardi, il écoute de la musique. Bof! La musique, c'est ennuyeux! (On Tuesday, he listens to music. It is nothing special. Music is boring!)

Mercredi, il joue au football. Bof! Le football, c'est difficile. (On Wednesday, he plays football. It is nothing special. Football's difficult.)

Jeudi, il joue du piano. Ah là là! Il déteste jouer du piano. (On Thursday, he plays the piano. Oh no. He hates playing the piano.)

Et vendredi? Qu'est-ce qu'il fait vendredi? Vendredi, il fait du vélo. Super, il adore faire du vélo! (And Friday? What does he do on Friday? On Friday, he goes cycling. Great, he loves going out on his bike!)

3. Tell the story. As they listen, pupils arrange their mini-cards in a line in the correct order on their desk. They could do this individually or in pairs.

4. Once everyone has placed their cards in sequence, check back by retelling the story, holding up your own cards at appropriate points.

 Écoutez bien l'histoire.   Listen carefully to the story.

Mettez les cartes dans le bon ordre.   Put the cards in the right order.

Comments

- For checking back, it would be useful if you had a set of A4 flashcards to show the class or fix to the board in the right sequence.
- As an alternative, give each pupil just one or two of the cards. Pupils listen to the story and hold their card in the air at the point their word or phrase is mentioned (or they could count how many times their word/phrase occurs in the story).

 With a more advanced class, use the game to practise speaking by asking volunteers to re-create the story, using their sequence of cards as a prompt.

Notes

....

....

....

....

....

....

....

....

....

....

14 Odd one out/ *Trouvez l'intrus*

Step by step

1. Divide the class into pairs or teams.
2. Say four words or phrases, three related and one that is not. For example, to practise rooms in the home, you might say:

   T: *A: la cuisine* (the kitchen), *B: la chambre* (the bedroom), *C: la tête* (the head), *D: la salle de bains* (the bathroom).

   Or for travel/transport, the phrases might be:

   T: *A: Je vais à l'école en voiture* (I go to school by car).

   B: Je prends le train pour aller en ville (I take the train to go to town).

   C: Je joue avec mes amis (I play with my friends).

   D: Je vais au jardin public à vélo (I go to the park on my bike).
3. Pupils write down the letter of the odd one out (in the examples above, this is C).
4. Pupils swap their papers with another pair or team to mark as you give the answers.

Classroom management	Whole class
Skill	Listening and concentration
Aim	To revise vocabulary
Resources	None

Useful phrases

Écoutez bien.

Quel mot/Quelle phrase ne va pas avec les autres ?

Listen carefully.

Which word/sentence doesn't go with the others?

Comments

- Add a writing and a speaking element to this game by getting pupils to make up their own odd-man-out puzzles to swap.

Increase the level of challenge by asking pupils to explain (in French or in English) why they made each choice. For the first example above, they could write *la tête, c'est une partie du corps* (the head is a part of the body) or *les autres sont des pieces/dans une maison* (the others are rooms/in a house).

15 Mystery voice/*La voix mystère*

Step by step

Classroom management	Whole class
Skill	Listening (and speaking)
Aim	To listen for – and spot – accuracy in grammar
Resources	Three chairs

1. Place three chairs at the front of the class, facing away from the pupils. Ask for three volunteers to sit on the chairs and be the 'judges'.

2. Ask a further volunteer to come to the front to be the 'voice'. She stands just behind the judges' backs, so the judges can't see who she is.

3. The voice makes a statement. She can say what she likes on a given topic, which should be one you have been working on recently or one you wish to revise. For example, if you have been working on the topic of school life, the pupil might say:

   P: *Je vais à l'école à pied* (I walk to school),

   or *J'aime les sciences, mais je n'aime pas le dessin* (I like science, but I don't like art),

   or *Ma matière préférée, c'est la musique* (My favourite subject is music).

4. The judges listen carefully to spot any slip-ups with grammar. They have thirty seconds to confer before giving their verdict. In that time, the rest of the pupils can also jot down any mistakes they spotted.

5. The voice goes back to her place in class and the judges turn to face the class and report back. They list any slip-ups they noticed. Ask the class if they agree with each one. If correct, the judges win a point. If incorrect, they lose a point. You will need to act as the adjudicator.

6. Award a bonus point if the judges can guess who the mystery voice was. This will lead to pupils disguising their voices, which can add to the fun.

Useful phrases		
Tu es la voix.	You are the voice [to a single pupil].
Dis une phrase sur [l'école].	Say one sentence about [school].
Vous êtes les juges.	You are the judges.
Écoutez bien la voix. Elle a fait des fautes ?	Listen carefully to the voice. Has she made any mistakes?

Comments

- Explain in advance that the voices need to keep their identity secret from the judges, and encourage them to disguise their voices by making them deeper, squeaky, etc.

 Increase the level of challenge by asking pupils to make up to five statements, depending on their ability.

Notes

16 Act it out/*Tous en scène*

Step by step

1. Prepare a short dialogue. This could be a recording, if you have audio equipment, or a text for you to read aloud.

   For example, if you are working on the topic of cafés, you could use a short jokey dialogue like this:

   Serveur: Une soupe … voilà ! (There you are … one soup!)

   Client: Mais c'est dégoûtant ! (But that's disgusting!)

   Serveur: Il y a un problème ? (Is there a problem?)

   Client: Il y a un insecte dans ma soupe. Regardez ! (There's an insect in my soup. Look!)

   Serveur: Pas de problème, il sait nager ! (No worries, it can swim!)

2. Divide the class into pairs.

3. Play the dialogue or read it aloud. Be sure you use a different voice for each speaker and add in plenty of expression – the more exaggerated the better! Check comprehension with questions in English or French.

4. Read the dialogue again several times. Encourage pupils to join in with you.

5. Once you feel the class knows the dialogue, discuss with them what makes a good performance (see below).

6. Let pupils practise acting out the dialogue in pairs.

7. Volunteers can come to the front to act out their dialogues.

Classroom management	Whole class, then pairs or small groups
Skill	Listening
Aim	To listen and memorise a short dialogue and act it out with appropriate expression and gestures
Resources	A short dialogue Optional: audio equipment

Useful phrases

Avez-vous bonne mémoire ?	Have you got good memories?
Écoutez et mémorisez le dialogue.	Listen and memorise the dialogue.
Ça a lieu (dans un café).	It takes place (in a café).
Maintenant, jouez le dialogue.	Now come and perform the dialogue.

Comments

- Discuss with pupils what make a good performance, e.g. bringing the words alive using tone of voice, facial expressions and gestures, speaking clearly and pronouncing the words well.

 For younger pupils, keep the dialogues very short, simple and repetitive. Older pupils can be challenged with longer texts.

Notes

17 Frog hunt/*La chasse aux grenouilles*

Step by step

1. This game needs to be played in a hall or playground. Divide the class into groups of three. Choose one group to be the three hunters.

2. Each of the remaining groups chooses one pupil to be the frog. The remaining two will be a lily pond. The groups stand spaced out across the hall.

Classroom management	Whole class
Skill	Listening
Aim	To listen for specific words or phrases
Resources	None

3. Tell pupils that when they hear you say a key word or phrase, all the frogs must leave their lily ponds and find a new one. It is the hunters' job to catch them while they are between ponds.

4. Tell pupils the key word(s) or phrase(s) they should listen out for. For example, you could choose days of the week, names of places around a town, or a phrase with a verb in the past tense, depending on what vocabulary you want them to listen to.

5. Call or read out a short text containing the words or phrases.

   For example:

   T: *Écoutez maintenant la semaine en couleurs* (Now listen to the week – in colours).

   Lundi gris, c'est reparti ! (Grey Monday, we're off again!)

   Ouvre les yeux, voici mardi bleu (Open your eyes, here's blue Tuesday).

   Tout est à l'envers, c'est mercredi vert (Everything's upside down, it's green Wednesday).

6. On hearing the trigger word/phrase, all the frogs move to a new, free lily pond and the hunters try to grab them. Once they reach the new lily pond, they swap, so that one of the others in the group becomes the frog for the next part of the game. If a frog is caught, he becomes a hunter.

7. The game continues with a new word or phrase as the trigger. You can play until all the frogs have been caught.

Useful phrases

Vous êtes les grenouilles.	You are the frogs.
Vous êtes les chasseurs.	You are the hunters.
Les chasseurs attrapent les grenouilles.	The hunters catch the frogs.

Comments

- It doesn't matter if pupils are not familiar with all the words they hear, so long as they are able to pick out the trigger ones.

 To make the game more challenging, you could add a speaking element: frogs that are caught can free themselves by repeating the trigger word or phrase, or by answering a question on the topic made up by the hunters.

Notes

....

....

....

....

....

....

....

....

....

....

....

....

....

....

....

....

....

18 Word by word/*Mot à mot*

Step by step

1. Before the lesson, choose a short song or poem with appropriate language. See page 245 for ideas. Write the words on a large sheet of paper (make copies – one per group) and then cut out the individual words (store these little pieces of paper in an envelope – one per group). The words could be from a song you have on audio, or one which you will sing to the class yourself.

Classroom management	Whole class/small groups
Skill	Listening and reading
Aim	To listen for specific words or phrases
Resources	Paper Envelopes Scissors (for teacher use) Optional: audio equipment if available

For example, for Hallowe'en, you could use this song, read aloud or sung to the tune of *Frère Jacques*:

T: *Hallowee-een, Hallowee-een*

C'est super, les sorcières

Donnez-nous des bonbons

Ou nous vous transformons

En dragon, en dragon.

(Hallowee-een, Hallowee-een, witches are great, give us some sweets or we'll turn you into a dragon.)

2. Divide the class into small groups and give each one an envelope containing the words.

3. Pupils empty the words onto the desk, face up.

4. Say or sing the song to the class at normal speed. (If you have an audio player, play the song instead.)

5. As they listen, the group arranges the words into the correct order.

6. Repeat the song as often as necessary, checking back each time to see if any of the groups have completed the song. You could do this competitively to see who can finish first.

Useful phrases

Écoutez bien la chanson/le poème.   Listen carefully to the song/poem.

Mettez les mots dans l'ordre.   Put the words in the right order.

Levez la main quand vous avez fini.   Put up your hand when you're finished.

Comments

- Be sure to check pupils' lyrics are correct. You could ask them to read the song/poem aloud if the language is familiar to them.
- After the game, pupils could learn the song or poem and say/sing it aloud.

 Provide more of a challenge by replacing one (or two) of the words in each envelope with a small piece of paper with a question mark on. Pupils will need to work out where to put the question mark and which word it stands for.

Notes

....

....

....

....

....

....

....

....

....

....

....

....

....

....

....

19 Mind the gap!/*Gare aux blancs !*

Step by step

Classroom management	Whole class
Skill	Listening, reading and writing
Aim	To revise vocabulary and to evaluate pupils' listening skills
Resources	Coloured felt-tips or chalk for writing on the board

1. Prepare a gapped text. You could base this on a song or poem (see page 245 for ideas), a text from a course book or a text you have written yourself.

   For example, if you are working on the topic of family, you might write:

   Salut ! Je m'appelle Lulu. Le ………. de mon ………., c'est mon ………. Il s'appelle Martin. Je n'ai pas de …………. Ma …………. s'appelle Anne. Elle a un …………, c'est mon …………. Il s'appelle David. J'ai aussi deux …………. et une ………….

2. Display the text on the board and give pupils a minute to look over it.

3. Divide the class into two teams. Give one team a red pen and the other a blue pen for writing on the board.

4. Read aloud the completed version of the text several times. For the gapped text above, you might read out:

   T: *Salut ! Je m'appelle Lulu. Le <u>père</u> de mon <u>père</u>, c'est mon <u>grand-père</u>. Il s'appelle Martin. Je n'ai pas de <u>grand-mère</u>. Ma <u>mère</u> s'appelle Anne. Elle a un <u>frère</u>, c'est mon <u>oncle</u>. Il s'appelle David. J'ai aussi deux <u>cousins</u> et une <u>cousine</u>.*

   (My father's father is my grandfather. His name is Martin. I haven't got a grandmother. My mother's name is Anne. She has one brother, that's my uncle. His name is David. I've also got two boy cousins and a girl cousin.)

5. A pupil from the blue team comes to the board and writes in one of the missing words using her blue pen. If it's correct, the word stays. If not, it is rubbed out.

6. Next, a pupil from the red team comes and writes in a word using his red pen. This is also accepted or rejected.

7. Repeat the process with different team members until the whole text is complete.

8. Read aloud the completed text and count up the number of words written in each colour. The team with the most points wins.

Useful phrases		
Viens au tableau.		Come to the board [to a single pupil].
Remplis un blanc.		Fill in one of the gaps [to a single pupil].

| *C'est au tour de l'autre équipe.* | It's the other team's turn. |
| *Quelle équipe a le plus de mots ?* | Which team has more words? |

Comments

- The words in the text do not need to be written in order (i.e., *Le p<u>ère</u> de mon p<u>ère</u>* does not have to be completed first).
- To support accurate spelling, you could display a list of family members on the board in random order.

 Introduce a speaking element by having pupils ask you questions to find out the missing words. For example:

P: *Qui est Anne ?* (Who is Anne?)

T: *La mère* (The mother).

Notes

....

....

....

....

....

....

....

....

....

....

....

....

20 Knock, knock/*Toc toc*

Step by step

Classroom management	Whole class
Skill	Listening
Aim	To spot mistakes while listening
Resources	Text containing deliberate mistakes

1. Prepare in advance a short text containing some deliberate mistakes. You could base this on a text from a course book or story book that pupils are already familiar with, or make up your own. For the activity to work, pupils need to be familiar with 99 per cent of the vocabulary.

   For example, if you are working on the topic of holidays, you could use a text like this:

   Quand je pars en vacances, je voyage en banane (When I go on holiday, I travel by banana).

   Le matin, je mange un bateau (In the mornings, I eat a boat).

   Il fait toujours beau – le ciel est bleu et le soleil est vert (The weather's always nice – the sky is blue and the sun is green).

   Je vais à la plage et je nage dans le ciel (I go to the beach and I swim in the sky).

   Je mange une glace au poisson (I eat a fish ice cream).

2. Make this a class v. teacher game. Read the text aloud to the class at a speed slightly slower than normal. Pupils knock on the desk if they hear something that is wrong. They win a point for a correct knock, but lose a point if they knock at the wrong place.

3. The class can win a bonus point if they can make a reasonable suggestion as to what the correct word might be; for example, *Quand je pars en vacances, je voyage en voiture/train/ avion/car* ... etc. (When I go on holiday, I travel by car/train/plane/coach ... etc.).

4. The class wins if they have more points than the teacher at the end of the game.

Useful phrases

Écoutez bien.	Listen carefully.
Frappez si vous entendez une erreur.	Knock if you hear a mistake.

Comments

- The game will be more fun if you make the mistakes a bit silly.
- Variation for pair-work practice: if you want to practise speaking/reading too, prepare two handouts of a text (A and B) that are slightly different. Each pupil in the pair has a different text and must not look at his partner's text. Pupil A reads his text aloud to Pupil B, who must spot the differences.

For older, more able pupils, you could make the mistakes more subtle.

Notes

Part 2: Speaking

To speak a foreign language well, you need plenty of practice. Repetition activities need not be boring, though. Games are not only fun and engaging; they provide a real reason to speak.

Some children love to speak up in class, while others are more shy. The games here are varied so that there are opportunities to speak in chorus, or in small groups and pairs, as well as in front of the whole class. Most of the games are for practising vocabulary pupils are already familiar with, rather than presenting new vocabulary.

Pupils need to develop accurate pronunciation and intonation so that others understand them when they are speaking or reading aloud. Playing with sounds (see page 211) can help with this.

A lot of the games in the other parts also provide opportunities for pupils to practise speaking. For example:

Part 1: Listening – games 11, 16, 20

Part 3: Reading – games 4, 10, 18, 20

Part 4: Writing – games 3, 11, 18, 20

Part 5: Numbers – games 3, 5–10, 12–14, 20

Part 6: Grammar – games 6, 7, 12–19.

1   The conductor/*Le chef d'orchestre*

Step by step

1. You are the conductor of an orchestra, and pupils are auditioning to join the orchestra.

2. First say the word or the phrase you want the pupils to repeat in a specific style (e.g. like a robot, whispering, etc.) and ask them to work out what it is. For example, if you want to practise greetings:

   T: [speaking like a robot] *Bonjour !*

   Class: You're speaking like a robot!

   T: *Oui ! Comme un robot.*

   Repeat this for all the different repetition styles you'd like to use. All pupils chorus the phrases after you, using the same voice/style.

3. Now play the audition game by pointing to individual pupils and modelling a style for them to copy, e.g.:

   T: [in a loud voice] *Salut ! Comment ça va ?*

   P1: [in a loud voice] *Salut ! Comment ça va ?*

   If the pupil repeats the words correctly using the correct voice, he comes to the front and joins the orchestra.

4. Ask the rest of the class to take part in the auditioning process by showing if they think the candidate did well (thumbs-up) or not (thumbs-down). Pupils who didn't repeat the words correctly stay back and have another chance later.

5. To round off in a fun way and signal the end of the game, ask *all* the pupils to repeat the words after you, but this time using different voices and styles ... Be warned, it might get noisy!

Classroom management	Whole class
Skill	Speaking
Aim	To repeat words or phrases in a fun and engaging way
Resources	Optional: a conductor's baton

Useful phrases

Dites/Dis .... comme un robot/une sorcière/un perroquet/une souris/un monstre !	Speak like ... a robot/a witch/a parrot/a mouse/a monster!
Parlez très fort/tout bas/vite/lentement.	Speak loudly/softly/fast/slowly.

Comments

- You can vary the format of this repetition game by having different groups of pupils repeating words at different times: in rows, pairs, only boys, only girls or in houses (if you have them at your school).

- If appropriate, let a volunteer take on the role of conductor.

 Vary the level of challenge by decreasing or increasing the speed at which you say the words or phrases, and giving pupils shorter or longer phrases to repeat.

Notes

_____

_____

_____

_____

_____

_____

_____

_____

_____

_____

_____

_____

_____

_____

2   Liar!/*Menteur !*

Step by step

The aim of the game is for pupils to repeat sentences only when they think they are true.

Classroom management	Whole class
Skill	Speaking (and listening)
Aim	To repeat words or phrases in a fun and engaging way
Resources	Optional: photos or flashcards

1.   Tell pupils to listen carefully to what you say. If what you say is true – and only if it is true – they must stand up and repeat what you said. If it is not true, they stay seated and say nothing. For example, to revise weather phrases, you could say:

T: *Il fait chaud aujourd'hui* (The weather's hot today).

The class must repeat the sentence *only* if it is a hot day – if not, they say nothing.

2.   Give pupils who get it wrong a chance to stay in the game: if they can repeat the next phrase correctly, they can carry on playing. If they don't, they become your spies, spotting who is not reacting correctly.

3.   The game continues until only one pupil is left (or, if you need to draw the game to a close, the winner could be the first pupil to react correctly).

> **Useful phrases**
>
> | | |
> |---|---|
> | *Écoutez et répétez si c'est vrai.* | Listen and repeat if it is true. |
> | *Levez-vous !* | Stand up! |
> | *Ne répétez pas si c'est faux.* | Don't repeat if it's false. |
> | *Restez assis.* | Stay in your seat. |

Comments

•   You could use photos or flashcards to revise different topics, for example clothing or hobbies. For example, show the class a photo of a person and say:

T: *Il porte un pantalon marron* (He's wearing brown trousers).

or *Il joue au football* (He's playing football).

As above, pupils only repeat when the sentence is true.

Add an extra linguistic challenge by asking pupils to produce a correct version of the false sentences, using negatives (*ne … pas (de)*) if appropriate.

T: *Il fait chaud aujourd'hui* (It's hot today).

Pupils: *Il ne fait pas chaud aujourd'hui* (It's not hot today) or *Il fait froid aujourd'hui* (It's cold today).

Notes

3 Feeling hot, hot, hot!/*Ça chauffe !*

Step by step

The aim of the game is to provide pupils with the opportunity to repeat language (especially vocabulary that can be chanted, e.g. numbers, days of the week, months of the year, time) in a fun way. The game can sometimes get a bit noisy!

Classroom management	Whole class/teams
Skill	Speaking
Aim	To repeat words by chanting
Resources	An object to hide (cuddly toy, ball, etc.)

1. Divide the class into two teams. A volunteer from Team A goes out of the room and the other pupils decide where to hide the object.

2. When the volunteer comes back into the classroom, her teammates start chanting the words you chose to practise. For example: *lundi, mardi, mercredi, jeudi, vendredi, samedi, dimanche* (Monday, Tuesday, Wednesday, Thursday, Friday, Saturday, Sunday).

3. As the volunteer moves around the classroom, her teammates chant more loudly as she gets nearer to where the object is hidden, and more quietly as she goes away from the object. Continue until the object is found (or set a time limit, e.g. a minute).

4. If the object is found, the volunteer scores a point for her team. If the object is not found within a given time, Team A scores no points.

5. A pupil from Team B is then chosen to go outside while pupils agree a new hiding place. The game continues as above.

Useful phrases

Faites deux équipes.	Make up two teams.
Un/e élève sort.	One pupil goes out.
Cachez l'objet !	Hide the object!
Il/Elle s'approche, parlez plus fort.	He/she is getting closer; speak more loudly.
Il/Elle s'éloigne, parlez plus bas.	He/she is getting further away; speak more softly.

Comments

- Adding rhythm can aid memory, so you could also turn this into a chant with finger clicks, claps, nods or stamping feet between each word:

  lundi (Monday) [click, click], *mardi* (Tuesday) [click, click] or for months of the year:

  janvier (January) [clap, clap], *février* (February) [clap, clap], *mars* (March) [clap, clap].

To challenge the teams, ask them to repeat the same sequence but in a different order, for example starting at the end: *dimanche, samedi, vendredi, ...* or *décembre, novembre, octobre, ...*

4 Secret signal/*Le détective*

Step by step

1. Write up or display on the board a list of words or phrases you want pupils to learn/revise. Make sure the class can all read and say the vocabulary to practise. This can be from any topic, for example, colours: *rouge* (red), *vert* (green), *bleu* (blue), *jaune* (yellow), etc.

Classroom management	Whole class
Skill	Speaking (also reading)
Aim	To repeat words by chanting
Resources	None

2. One pupil volunteers to be the detective and leaves the room.

3. The rest of the class agrees on a secret signal (e.g. scratching their head, puffing up their cheeks, biting their bottom lip).

4. Choose one pupil to give the secret signal. Each time she gives the signal, the class must chant a different word from the board:

   Class: *Rouge, rouge, rouge, rouge* ... [secret signal]. *Vert, vert, vert* ... [secret signal]. *Bleu, bleu, bleu*, etc.

5. Ask the detective to come back into the room while the class is saying the first word from the list over and over again. When the class sees the secret signal, they move on to the next word/phrase in the list.

6. The detective tries to work out who is giving the secret signal. When he does, he then names the next detective to go out of the room. Repeat the process, changing the secret signal each time.

Répétez les mots/les phrases.	Repeat the words/sentences.
Qui veut être détective ?	Who wants to be the detective?
Choisissez un signal secret.	Choose a secret signal.
Répétez tous ensemble.	Repeat all together.

Comments

- You could play a variation of this game called *le tic-tic*. One pupil volunteers to be the detective and goes out of the room. The class is divided into pairs. Each pair chooses a different word on the board. Both pupils in the pair repeat their phrase while mingling among the rest of the class in the classroom. The detective comes back, and his mission is to listen carefully to what pupils are saying and to find the matching pairs.

Set a time limit, after which you count how many pairs he managed to make. Repeat the whole procedure with a new detective, and with different pairs/words each time.

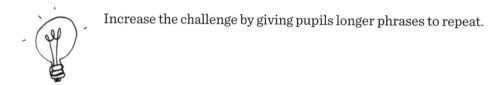 Increase the challenge by giving pupils longer phrases to repeat.

Notes

....

....

....

....

....

....

....

....

....

....

....

....

....

....

....

....

5 Gossip/*Petits potins*

Step by step

1. This game is based on the well-known game of Chinese whispers. Divide the class into several teams (the more pupils in a team the better, as the message is more likely to become distorted, which will make the activity more fun). Each team lines up.

Classroom management	Whole class/teams
Skill	Speaking
Aim	To repeat words/phrases
Resources	None

2. Explain that you are going to whisper a message to the last pupil in each row. When you give the signal, each pupil in turn must whisper the message to the pupil in front of him. This continues down the line.

3. Go to the end of each line and whisper the same word/message to the last person in each line.

4. Pupils whisper the message to the person standing in front of them, who then whispers it to the next pupil and so on. No one else must hear!

5. When the person at the front of the line gets the message, she must say it aloud. Have any of the teams managed to transmit the original message?

Useful phrases

Écoutez bien et répétez le message.	Listen carefully and repeat the message.
Chuchote/Chuchotez !	Whisper!
Dis/ Dites le message tout haut.	Say the message aloud.
C'est/Ce n'est pas le bon message !	The message is/isn't correct!

Comments

- This game is also known as Grapevine, Secret message, Telephone or *le téléphone arabe* in French.
- If you have access to audio equipment, you could play some French music in the background to make it harder for others to hear what is being whispered.

Increase the challenge by making the game competitive: pupils repeat the phrase as quickly as they can, and the first team to say the correct message aloud wins a point.

Increase the level of linguistic challenge by increasing the length of the secret message. For example, if you are revising animals, say: *Un lapin* (a rabbit), or *J'ai un lapin* (I've got a rabbit), or *Susie a un petit lapin gris* (Susie has a little grey rabbit), or *Lucas a deux chiens noirs et un petit chat qui s'appelle Mistigri* (Lucas has two black dogs and a little cat called Mistigri).

Notes

....

....

....

....

....

....

....

....

....

....

....

....

....

....

6   Describe and draw/*Le dessin-mystère*

Step by step

1. Draw a simple picture and place it on your desk. The class must not see it. For example, if you want to revise prepositions of place (over, under, beside, next to) and animals, you could draw the picture below.

2. Divide the class into teams.

3. The first pupil in each team runs forward to look at the picture. He then goes back and tells the second in line one element of the picture, who then passes this information to the third, and so on down the line. The last person in the line must draw it. Repeat this procedure until the picture is complete. For example:

   P1: *Il y a une table* (There's a table).

   P2: *Sur la table, il y a un chat* (On the table, there is a cat).

   P3: *Sous la table, il y a un chien* (Under the table, there is a dog).

4. The first team to complete the picture as accurately as possible wins.

Classroom management	Whole class/teams
Skill	Speaking
Aim	To make up phrases
Resources	Simple hand-drawn pictures Paper and pen per team for pupils to draw with

Useful phrases

Viens voir l'image.	Come and see the picture.
Décris l'image.	Describe the picture.
Dessine l'image.	Draw the picture.

Comments

- As for the game of Gossip (page 49), you could play some French music in the background to make it harder for pupils to hear what the other teams are whispering.

- If the pupil drawing needs help, she must pass a message back up the line to the first pupil, who must answer by passing a message down the line.

Increase the level of challenge by drawing more complicated scenes.

7 Spelling race/*La course aux mots*

Step by step

1. Before playing the game, revise the alphabet by singing an ABC song if your pupils know one, or going round the class in a Mexican wave (see page 54).

2. Write or display a short text on the board. It does not have to be a text where your pupils understand every word. You could use, for example a

Classroom management	Whole class/pair-work
Skill	Speaking (and listening and reading)
Aim	To practise spelling using the alphabet
Resources	Optional: a text

short text from a story book or a textbook, a poem, a nursery rhyme, a song, or a text written by a pupil. You could even choose a selection of words which look similar to each other, e.g. which all start with the same letter or with similar sounds, or make up your own nonsense sentences:

- *Ma maman et Mamie Manon sont maintenant dans la maison* (My mum and Granny Manon are now in the house).

- *Mon amie Amélie aime amener ses amies chez son aimable mamie* (My friend Amélie likes taking her friends to visit her nice granny).

3. Pupils play the game in pairs. One pupil looks at the text and selects a word. He starts to spell it. His partner listens carefully and tries to name the word before the spelling is finished in order to win a point.

   P1: *m – a*

   P2: *Mamie !*

   P1: *Non ! Alors, m – a – m*

   P2: *Maman !*

   P1: *Oui, c'est maman. Tu as gagné. À ton tour.*

4. Pupils swap roles and repeat the activity several times. In order to win, the speller needs to speed up their spelling. The winner is the pupil with most points after a set time.

> **Useful phrases**

Regardez le texte.	Look at the text.
Choisissez un mot.	Choose a word.
Épelez le mot.	Spell the word.
Tu as gagné.	You've won.
À mon/ton tour.	It's my/your turn.

Comments

- You may want pupils to spell words with accents. If so, practise naming the accents and symbols first:

  é: e accent aigu

  è: e accent grave

  ë: e accent tréma

  ê: e accent circonflexe

  œ: o et e collés

  ç: c cédille

You could increase the level of challenge by asking pupils to spell a word backwards.

As a variation, show the text to the class, then ask the pupil who is going to name the word being spelled to close her eyes or turn away from the text. She then has to concentrate more on listening to the spelling while trying to recall the words she saw in the text.

Notes

....

....

....

....

....

....

....

....

....

....

....

8   Mexican wave/*La ola*

Step by step

The aim of this game is to provide pupils with the opportunity to learn and practise vocabulary that can be chanted (alphabet, numbers, days of the week, months of the year, seasons, time, colours, greetings, action verbs, and so on) in a fun way.

Classroom management	Whole class/teams
Skill	Speaking
Aim	To chant words/phrases as part of a sequence
Resources	Vocabulary list

1. First, go through the list of vocabulary you want to practise with the whole class, using choral repetition.

2. When pupils are familiar with the words, ask them to do a Mexican wave: they have to say the next letter/number/day of the week/month while standing and throwing their arms in the air.

3. Divide the class into three or four teams. Each team has a go at saying the sequence of words, each pupil saying a different word in order, for example:

    P1: *lundi*

    P2: *mardi*

    P3: *mercredi*, etc.

4. If one of the pupils cannot provide the next word in the sequence, his team loses a point and another team has a go.

Useful phrases

Faites une ola avec (les jours de la semaine).	Do a Mexican wave with (the days of the week).
Levez-vous.	Stand up.
Levez les bras.	Put your arms in the air.
Perdu ! Recommencez !	You've lost! Start again!
C'est bien ! Bravo !	That's good! Well done!

Comments

*   You could play a variation of the Mexican wave using flashcards: give each pupil in a team a flashcard with one of the words of the sequence you want to practise. Pupils take turns to hold their card above their head and say the word or phrase. Once a sequence has been completed, give a signal. Every pupil then passes their card to the pupil on their right and repeat the procedure.

Vary the activity by asking pupils to make the wave go in the opposite direction whenever they hear your signal (hand clap, whistle, bell, etc.).

Increase the linguistic challenge by asking pupils in each team to say small chunks of longer sentences (relating to the topic you are working on) rather than individual words.

For example:

Il/habite/dans/une/petite/maison/au/centre-ville.
(He lives in a small house in the town centre.)

Je voudrais/une glace/au chocolat/et à la vanille/s'il vous plaît.
(I would like a chocolate and vanilla ice cream please.)

Elle/n'aime pas/jouer au/football/mais/elle adore/jouer au tennis.
(She doesn't like playing football but she loves playing tennis.)

Notes

....

....

....

....

....

....

....

....

....

....

....

....

9 Flashcard auction/*Cartes aux enchères*

Step by step

The aim of the game is to introduce and practise new language. This works for any topic.

Classroom management	Whole class/teams
Skill	Speaking
Aim	To learn and practise new language orally
Resources	Flashcards (relevant to your topic)

1. Prepare a series of flashcards on a topic. For example, if you are working on ways of getting around, you might have *une voiture* (a car), *un car* (a coach), *un bus* (a bus), *un bateau* (a boat), *un avion* (a plane), *un train* (a train), *un métro* (an underground train), etc.

2. Divide the class into teams of five or six.

3. Show the class the first flashcard. Say the word/phrase represented several times, e.g.

   T: [holding up flashcard of car] *Une voiture. Une voiture. Une voiture.*

4. Ask each team to decide how many of them they think will be able to repeat the word correctly. Give them a minute or so to discuss, during which you carry on repeating the word.

5. Each team then bids that number (which determines the number of points they will score if all the pupils nominated do in fact say the words correctly).

6. In turn, the nominated pupils say the word or phrase. If one doesn't say it correctly, give her three more chances. Her team members are allowed to help.

7. Repeat for all the flashcards and total up the points. The team with most points wins.

> **Useful phrases**
>
> *Faites des équipes.* — Make up teams.
>
> *Combien d'élèves parlent dans votre équipe ?* — How many pupils will speak in your team?
>
> *X points pour votre équipe.* — X points for your team.

Comments

- Using the idea of bidding for a card gives less confident pupils the chance to have a go when they feel ready, and giving them three tries encourages everyone to have a go.

- You can vary the game from step 3 when practising or revising language, by adding an element of speed:

  - Play Slow reveal: place a sheet of paper over the flashcard to hide it, and reveal it slowly. Which team bids for it first? They win the card if all pupils name it correctly.

- Play Through the keyhole: cut a keyhole shape in a sheet of paper and move it over the flashcard. Once pupils have had a chance to glimpse the picture and think they know what it is, teams put in their bids as fast as possible.
- Play Flash: you show each card to the class for a second only.

Increase the level of challenge by showing several cards in a sequence. Each team must not only recall the correct words, but in the correct order.

For example:

P: *Un bus, une voiture, un car et un train* (A bus, a car, a coach and a train).

Increase the level of linguistic challenge by asking pupils to include the words/phrases on each card in a sentence. For example:

P: [After seeing the card with a car] *C'est une voiture (bleue)* (It's a (blue) car).

Notes

....

....

....

....

....

....

....

....

....

....

....

....

10 Mind reading/*Télépathie*

Step by step

1. Prepare some flashcards: for example, pictures showing rooms in a house: *la chambre* (the bedroom), *la cuisine* (the kitchen), *le salon* (the sitting-room), *la salle à manger* (the dining room), *la salle de bains* (the bathroom), etc.

2. Show all the flashcards to the class, naming each one.

3. Shuffle the cards and place them in a pile on your desk, face down.

4. Take a flashcard from the pile and hold it with the picture facing you, so the class can't see what it is.

5. Ask pupils if they can read your mind and say which picture they think you are looking at. They put up their hands to guess. The first pupil with his hand up goes first. If he guesses correctly, give his team a point; if not, ask a different team. Pupils must listen carefully to each other's guesses in order to avoid repeating a guess that has already been rejected.

6. Limit the number of guesses pupils can have. For example, if they haven't guessed after three tries, you score a point. Which team will win? Or will the teacher beat them all?

Classroom management	Whole class
Skill	Speaking (and listening)
Aim	To revise known language orally
Resources	Flashcards (relevant to your topic)

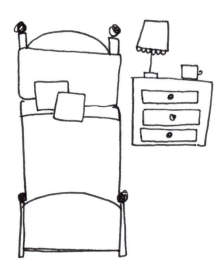

> **Useful phrases**

Faites des équipes.	Make up teams.
Qu'est-ce que c'est ?	What is it?
Oui, c'est ça !	Yes, you're right!
Non, ce n'est pas ça.	No, it's not that.

Comments

- To add fun, you could use an idea from page 249, like 'Walking the plank'.

- As a variation, pupils can play 'Poker face' in pairs. Make sets of mini-flashcards and hand them out to each pair. Pupil A takes a card and keeps it hidden from Pupil B. Then she names it, e.g. *C'est le salon* (It's the sitting-room). Pupil B must decide whether Pupil A is telling the truth or bluffing, saying: *C'est vrai/C'est faux* (It's true/false). If B is right, A says *'Gagné'* and hands the card to B. If B is wrong, A says *'Perdu'* and keeps the card.

 To increase the level of linguistic challenge, pupils win an extra point if they use the word in a sentence. For example, if they guessed you were holding the sitting-room card, they could say: *Je suis dans le salon* (I'm in the sitting-room), *Je regarde la télé dans le salon* (I watch TV in the sitting-room), etc.

Notes

....

....

....

....

....

....

....

....

....

....

....

....

....

11 Play for points/*Le score mystère*

Step by step

1. Before pupils arrive, write random numbers on the board. Use adhesive tack to stick a flashcard over each one. For example, to revise hobbies, you could have pictures to represent the following: *je fais du vélo* (I ride a bike), *je regarde la télé* (I watch TV), *je joue à des jeux vidéo* (I play video games), *je promène le chien* (I walk the dog), *je joue du piano* (I play the piano), *je lis* (I read), etc.

Classroom management	Whole class/teams
Skill	Speaking
Aim	To practise known language orally
Resources	Flashcards (relevant to your topic) Adhesive tack

2. When pupils arrive, divide them into teams.

3. The teams take turns to nominate a pupil to say the phrase associated with one of the flashcards. If he is correct, he can remove that flashcard to reveal the number of points he has won for his team.

   The winning team is the one with the most points once all the flashcards have been removed.

> **Useful phrases**
>
> | *Faites des équipes.* | Divide into teams. |
> |---|---|
> | *Un(e) élève choisit une carte.* | One pupil chooses a card. |
> | *Il/elle dit une phrase pour la carte.* | He/she says a sentence to describe the card. |
> | *Gagnez des points !* | Win some points! |

Comments

- For cross-curricular work with maths, replace the numbers with simple sums which pupils have to work out (in French!) to find out how many points they score. For example, *deux plus trois, sept moins quatre, vingt-cinq divisé par cinq* (two plus three, seven minus four, twenty-five divided by five).

- You could include negative numbers on the board, so that a team's score could go down as well as up!

 To increase the level of challenge, replace the flashcards in a different order on top of the numbers. Pupils must try to remember where the highest numbers were and choose the corresponding flashcards.

12 Heads or tails/*Pile ou face*

Step by step

Warning: this game requires quite a bit of preparation.

Classroom management	Pair-work
Skill	Speaking
Aim	To revise known language from several topics orally
Resources	Mini-flashcards Envelopes Coins Joker cards (see page 250)

1. Prepare a series of mini-flashcards to revise two or more topics, for example, rooms in a house and animals. Make enough sets for pupils to work in pairs. Divide each set of cards into two, placing half in an envelope marked '*PILE*' (tails) and the other half in an envelope marked '*FACE*' (heads).

2. Pupils work in pairs. Hand out a set of mini-flashcards to each pair as well as a coin (ideally, use plastic euros if you have a set).

3. Pupils take turns to toss the coin, taking a card from the corresponding envelope. If Pupil 1 names the card correctly, she wins it. If she can't name it and Pupil 2 can, Pupil 2 wins it instead. For example:

   P1: [tosses coin] *Pile* (Tails). [takes bedroom card from '*PILE*' set] *La chambre.*

   P2: *Oui, tu gagnes la carte* (Yes, you win the card).

   or

   P1: [tosses coin] *Face* (Heads). [picks cat card from '*FACE*' set] *Le chien* (the dog).

   P2: *Non ! C'est le chat* (No, it's the cat).

4. The game continues until all the cards have been used. The winner is the pupil with the most cards.

Useful phrases

Jouez à deux.	Play in pairs.
Tirez à pile ou face.	Toss a coin.
Tirez une carte de la bonne enveloppe.	Take a card from the right envelope.

Comments

- While pupils are playing, walk around the class with a set of joker cards. If a pupil can't name a card, she can ask you for a joker card. Stop all play in the class while the pupil nominates another pupil to help her (a bit like Phone-a-friend). If the friend gives a correct answer, he gets the joker card and an additional point and the first pupil gets to keep the mini-card. If the friend can't name the card either, the first pupil loses a turn.

- A variation is to use one or two dice in order to select a card from a set of six or twelve mini-cards. Each pair sets out their six (or twelve) cards on their desk and numbers them 1–6 (or 1–12). They take turns throwing a die (or two dice) in order to pick a card. They must then name it correctly in order to keep it.

 Increase the level of challenge by asking pupils to include the word or phrase relating to the card, in a sentence of varying length according to the level of the class. For example, for the word '*salon*': *C'est le salon* (It's the sitting-room), *J'aime bien le salon* (I like the sitting-room), *Le chat est dans le salon* (The cat is in the sitting-room).

Notes

....

....

....

....

....

....

....

....

....

....

....

13 Kim's game/*Le jeu de Kim*

Step by step

1. Bring in a bag containing a number of small objects or flashcards. One by one, take them out of the bag and ask pupils if they can name them:

   T: *Qu'est-ce que c'est ?* (What's this?)

   If they don't remember the French word, tell them.

2. When the bag is empty, count the items or cards back in, asking the class to name them again.

Classroom management	Whole class/small groups/ pairs
Skill	Speaking (also observation and memory skills)
Aim	To revise vocabulary orally
Resources	A bag with small objects (eraser, pencil, etc.) or series of flashcards and adhesive tack

3. Next, remove all the objects and place them on the desk or stick the cards to the board with adhesive tack. Pupils gather round the desk or study the board in silence for up to twenty seconds.

4. Pupils all close their eyes. You remove one or two of the objects/cards.

5. Pupils open their eyes and say which objects/cards are missing.

6. Once the game is familiar, let a volunteer take on your role and ask the questions.

Useful phrases

Qu'est-ce que c'est ?	What's this?
Regardez bien !	Look carefully!
Fermez les yeux !	Shut your eyes!
Qu'est-ce qui manque ?	What's missing?

Comments

- Instead of removing objects/cards while pupils have their eyes closed, you could *add* one or two. Can pupils say which items are new?

- You can play a variation of this game even if you have no objects or cards to hand. Just read out a list of familiar words or phrases you'd like pupils to practise. Then read your list aloud a second time, but this time miss out one word or phrase. Can pupils supply the missing word or phrase?

- To add in some reading practice, you could write a series of words or phrases on the board in random order. Ask pupils to close their eyes and rub out two of the words/phrases. Can they remember which have disappeared?

Challenge pupils' sense of observation by laying out the objects/cards in a certain order. While pupils look away, change the order. Can they recall the original sequence? Ask a volunteer to say all the names in the correct order.

Increase the level of linguistic challenge by adding in adjectives of description, e.g. *une petite gomme blanche* (a small white eraser), *une grande gomme jaune* (a big yellow eraser), etc.

Notes

....

....

....

....

....

....

....

....

....

....

....

....

....

....

....

....

14 The question race/*Le relais des questions*

Step by step

1. Prepare a series of questions. It could be on any topic. For example, for practising or revising personal details: *Tu t'appelles comment ?* (What is your name?), *Tu as quel âge ?* (How old are you?), *C'est quand, ton anniversaire ?* (When's your birthday?), *Tu as des frères et sœurs ?* (Have you got any brothers and sisters?), *Tu habites où ?* (Where do you live?), etc.

Classroom management	Whole class
Skill	Speaking (and listening)
Aim	To practise asking questions as well as answering
Resources	None

2. Divide the class into two teams and line each team up, one pupil behind another, in front of the board.

3. Ask the first pupil at the top of each line a question. Pupil 1 answers the question then asks it to the next pupil in the line, who answers it and then passes it on to the next pupil, and so on until it reaches the last pupil in the line.

    Pupil 1 [to Pupil 2]: *Tu t'appelles comment ?*

    Pupil 2: *Je m'appelle Lucie.* [turns to Pupil 3]: *Tu t'appelles comment ?* etc.

4. When the last pupil has answered, he rushes to the front of the line to get another question from you and the same process is repeated with that question.

5. The winning team is the one who answers the most questions.

Useful phrases

Faites deux équipes.	Make two teams.
Écoutez la question et répondez.	Listen to the question and answer it.
Tournez-vous et posez la question.	Turn round and ask the question.

Comments

*   Play a variation of this game with younger pupils: The teddy race (*La course des nounours*). The principle is the same, but pupils simply have to repeat a word or a phrase while passing a teddy (or a ball) down the line. For example:

    P1: *Je m'appelle Ben.*

    P2: *Je m'appelle Lucie.*

    P3: *Je m'appelle Alex.*

    A team wins when their teddy is the first to reach the top of the line again.

- Another simpler variation is Beat the clock (*Contre la montre*), when you time how long each team takes to pass a word/phrase/sentence along the line while still pronouncing the words correctly.

 To increase the level of challenge, you could set a timer. Pupils will then have to ask and answer questions down the line as fast as they can in order to answer as many questions as possible in that given time.

Notes

....

....

....

....

....

....

....

....

....

....

....

....

....

....

....

....

....

....

15 I went to market/*Au marché, j'ai acheté*

Step by step

This is a traditional memory or cumulative game often used to practise lexical sets.

Classroom management	Whole class
Skill	Speaking (also listening and memorising)
Aim	To practise and revise vocabulary orally
Resources	None

1. First, remind pupils of the vocabulary you want to revise.

2. Start the game by providing the first part of a sentence to be completed. This will depend on the vocabulary you wish to practise. Remind pupils that they need to say « *et* » (and) before the last item in the list.

3. Pupil 1 completes your sentence using an item from the vocabulary you wish to revise. Pupil 2 repeats it and adds another item. Pupil 3 starts from the beginning and adds a third item, etc.

    T: *Au marché, j'achète …* (At the market, I buy …)

    P1: *Au marché, j'achète des pommes* (apples).

    P2: *Au marché, j'achète des pommes et des poires* (and pears).

    P3: *Au marché, j'achète des pommes, des poires et des abricots* (and apricots).

4. When a pupil is unable to repeat or add a new item to the list, she is out. The winner is the last pupil standing.

Useful phrases

Écoutez le début de la phrase. Listen to the start of the sentence.

Répétez tout et ajoutez quelque chose. Repeat everything and add something.

Comments

- A variation is to play the game in teams and to provide each team with a number of joker cards (see page 250). Rather than eliminating a pupil who can't remember existing items, or add a new item, encourage collaboration by allowing the team to play a joker which allows them to help their teammate by miming, mouthing the word silently, spelling the word in the air, etc.

- This game can be adapted for use with different levels and lexical sets as follows:

  Holiday clothes: *Dans ma valise, il y a* (In my suitcase there is …) *un short, un t-shirt,* etc.

  Parts of the body: *J'ai mal à la tête* (My head hurts), *au dos* (my back hurts), *aux pieds* (my feet hurt).

  Transport: *Je voyage* (I travel by) *en train/en bus/en taxi/à pied* (on foot)/*à vélo* (by bike).

  Sports: *Au centre sportif* (At the sports centre) *je fais du judo* (I do judo), *je joue au foot* (I play football).

 Increase the level of linguistic challenge by adapting the starter sentence to suit the level of the class. For example, if using the topic of food, you could change tenses and say: *Au marché, j'achète …* (At the market, I buy …), *Je vais au marché et j'achète …* (I go to the market and buy …), *Je suis allé(e) au marché et j'ai acheté …* (I went to the market and I bought …).

Notes

....

....

....

....

....

....

....

....

....

16 Spot the star/*Où est la star ?*

Step by step

1. Ask for a volunteer to be a 'journalist' and send her outside the room. Tell her she will need to ask the class for their names in order to find the star (choose a French celebrity) when she returns.

2. Ask for a volunteer to be the star. Choose a French celebrity (such as a footballer, actor or singer). Show a photo of them if you have one available.

Classroom management	Whole class
Skill	Speaking (and listening)
Aim	To practise asking and answering questions
Resources	A timer Optional: photos of French celebrities

3. When the volunteer comes back into the room, the 'journalist' circulates and asks questions. Set a time limit, say two minutes, to find the star.

    Pupil 1 (journalist): *Comment tu t'appelles ?*

    P2: *Je m'appelle Lucie.*

    P1: *Et toi, comment tu t'appelles ?*

    P3: *Je m'appelle <name of star>.*

    P1: *Trouvé !*

4. When the star is found, stop the clock. Send another journalist out and nominate a new star. Repeat the same process. The winner is the journalist who found the star in the shortest time.

Qui veut être journaliste ?	Who wants to be a journalist?
Qui veut être la star ?	Who wants to be the star?
Trouvé !	Found you!

Useful phrases

Comments

- If you want the game to go faster, send several 'journalists' out and have several 'stars' among the remaining pupils.

To increase the challenge, ask pupils to have a longer dialogue, using greetings and expressions of politeness:

P1: (journalist): *Bonjour. Ça va ?* (Hello, how are you?)

P2: *Ça va, merci* (Fine, thanks).

P1: *Comment tu t'appelles ?*

P2: *Je m'appelle ...*

P1: *D'accord, merci. Au revoir !* (OK, thanks. Bye!)

P2: *De rien ! Au revoir.* (Don't mention it. Bye!)

Notes

....

....

....

....

....

....

....

....

....

....

....

....

....

....

17 Old maid/*Le pouilleux*

Step by step

This game can be used as a plenary at the end of a topic to assess what has been learned, or at any point in a sequence of lessons to check learning up to that point. It can be used for any topic.

Classroom management	Whole class
Skill	Speaking
Aim	To revise the language of a topic orally
Resources	Two sets of cards

1. Prepare two sets of cards, one with the French words/phrases/sentences to be revised and the other set with their translation in English. You need enough to give each pupil two cards – one of each. Insert two cards that do not make a matching pair (pupils who end up with those will be the old maids/*pouilleux,* which, in French, means fleabag!).

2. Hand out two cards to each pupil, one from each set. Pupils then mill around. They call their French phrases aloud in order to find the child with the matching translation.

For example:

P1: *Je joue du piano* (I play the piano).

P2: *I play the saxophone. Ce n'est pas ça ...* (that's not it). *Je joue de la flûte.*

P1: *I play the flute. C'est ça ! Voilà la carte* (That's it! Here's your card).

3. Pupils with an English translation give their card to the pupil who has the matching French card. At the end of the game, there should be two pupils left without a matching card. They are the *pouilleux.*

4. Collect all the cards, shuffle them and redistribute them for another game. Repeat the same process as above. Remove the non-matching cards and insert two different ones.

Useful phrases	*Lisez les cartes en français.*	Read the cards in French.
	Trouvez les mêmes cartes en anglais.	Find the matching cards in English.
	Tu es le pouilleux !	You are the old maid!

Comments

- You could play a similar game with word cards and picture cards with younger pupils; in this game, insert one picture card which does not have a corresponding word card and vice versa.

 To increase the challenge, ask pupils to learn the phrases on their cards and say them from memory.

Notes

....

....

....

....

....

....

....

....

....

....

....

....

....

....

....

18 Guess the question/*C'est quoi, la question ?*

Step by step

This game can be used as a plenary at the end of a lesson and can be used for any topic.

Classroom management	Whole class/groups
Skill	Speaking
Aim	To ask questions on one or more topics
Resources	Cards

1. Prepare several sets of cards with words or phrases you want pupils to revise.

   For example: *dix ans* (ten years old), *un chien* (a dog), *deux sœurs* (two sisters), *du violon* (violin), *le vert* (green), *l'anglais* (English), *le tennis* (tennis).

2. Divide the class into groups. Give each group a set of cards.

3. One pupil picks up a card from the pile and the group comes up with a question that you might ask to get that answer.

   For example:

   P1 [reading the card]: *Dix ans.*

   P2: *Tu as quel âge ?* (How old are you?)

4. When they come up with a correct question, they win the card. The group with the most cards wins.

Useful phrases

Regardez les cartes.	Look at the cards.
Lisez les réponses.	Read the answers.
Trouvez les questions.	Find the questions.
Gagné ! / Perdu !	You win!/You lose!
Recommencez.	Start again.

Comments

- If you give each group the same set of cards, they will have to work quietly so they are not overheard by other groups.
- If you give each group a different set of cards, they can exchange their cards until all the groups have played with all the cards.

- A card-free variation is to play this game orally with the whole class. Pupils take turns to suggest an answer which they write down secretly on a piece of paper. The rest of the class has to work out the question the pupil had in mind. For example:

P1: *C'est en février* (It's in February).

Class: *C'est quand, ton anniversaire ?* (When's your birthday?)

P1: *Non, ce n'est pas ça* (No, that's not it).

They keep trying until someone comes up with the right question, e.g.:

Class: *C'est quand, la Saint-Valentin ?* (When's Valentine's day?)

P1: *Oui, c'est ça !* (That's it!)

Whoever comes up with the correct question scores a point.

To increase the challenge, use a timer and set a time limit.

Notes

....

....

....

....

....

....

....

....

....

....

....

19 Pictionary/*Le pictionnaire*

Step by step

This game is based on Pictionary, the guessing game invented by Canadian Robert Angel in 1985. The aim is to guess the word/phrase drawn by your team members. Choose this game to revise lexical items that are easily drawn.

Classroom management	Whole class/teams
Skill	Speaking (also listening and making deductions)
Aim	To practise language from any topic orally
Resources	Pen to draw on board

1. Prepare a list of words from lexical areas you want to practise/revise, such as food, animals, clothes, sports, parts of the body, places in town, etc.
2. Divide the class into two teams.
3. One pupil from Team A comes to the board. Whisper a word in her ear. She starts drawing it. Point out that the person drawing cannot use letters or numbers.
4. When a team member has named the item correctly, the team wins a point. Another pupil from the team comes to the board. Repeat the same process.
5. If no member from Team A can name the drawing, Team B can have a go. If they give a correct answer, they win two points.
6. Repeat the same process with Team B. The team with the most points wins.

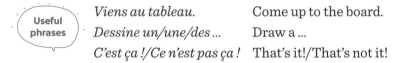

Useful phrases		
Viens au tableau.	Come up to the board.
Dessine un/une/des …	Draw a …
C'est ça !/Ce n'est pas ça !	That's it!/That's not it!

Comments

- A variation of this game can be played in pairs with pupils drawing on their partner's back with their finger, or simply drawing in the air.

Increase the challenge by limiting the drawing time (e.g. twenty seconds).

You can also make the game more challenging by suggesting lexical items that are not so easy to draw, such as rooms, hobbies, school subjects or shops.

20 The thingummyjig/*Le schmilblick*

Step by step

This game is based on a French TV show from the early 1970s called *Le Schmilblick* (a made-up word) in which candidates had to guess the name of an object. It is more suited to older, more able learners.

Classroom management	Whole class
Skill	Speaking (also reading and listening)
Aim	To revise nouns (and ask questions)
Resources	List of words

1. Prepare two lists of nouns you would like pupils to revise.

2. Divide the class into two teams. Give each team a list.

3. Team A chooses their first 'schmilblick' from the words listed. Meanwhile, Team B prepares a list of questions to find out what word 'schmilblick' stands for. Team A can only answer *oui* (yes) or *non* (no), so the questions need to be drawn up with that in mind.

4. Pupils from Team B ask their questions.

   For example:

   Team B: *Le schmilblick est une personne ?* (Is the thingummyjig a person?)

   Team A: *Non.*

   Team B: *C'est un animal ?* (Is it an animal?)

   Team A: *Oui,* etc.

5. Set a timer. If Team B hasn't guessed the 'schmilblick' within the set time, they lose.

6. Team B now chooses a 'schmilblick' and Team A will ask questions. The team who makes the most correct guesses within the time limit wins.

> **Useful phrases**

Choisissez un mot-schmilblick.	Choose a word for the thingummyjig.
Posez des questions.	Ask questions.
Répondez par « oui » ou par « non ».	Answer 'yes' or 'no'.

Comments

• With a more advanced class, play a whole-class variation of this game in which pupils take turns to use the word *schmilblick* in a sentence. The other players make guesses.

   For example:

   P1: *Je mange un schmilblick tous les jours* (I eat a *schmilblick* every day).

   P2: *Un fruit ?*

P1: *Non.*

P3: *Un sandwich ?*

P1: *Oui !*

 To increase the challenge, don't give a list of specific words but let pupils decide what their *schmilblick* will be.

Notes

....

....

....

....

....

....

....

....

....

....

....

....

....

....

....

....

Part 3: Reading

This part of the book focuses on another key skill for the young learner: reading. Being able to link the sound, spelling and meaning of a word or phrase in another language needs constant practice.

Here, we include games at a word, sentence and text level, encouraging pupils to read carefully and show their understanding of words, phrases and simple writing.

The activities show that reading can be fun as well as functional. Poems, rhymes and songs are perfect for this. There are some examples you could use on page 245.

Some of the games in other parts of the book also have a reading element, or could be adapted to include one:

Part 1: Listening – games 1, 6, 14, 18, 19

Part 2: Speaking – games 7, 11, 13, 17

Part 4: Writing – games 3, 10, 11, 15, 16, 18, 19.

1   Don't cross the line!/
Ne traverse pas la ligne!

Step by step

Classroom management	Whole class/teams
Skill	Reading
Aim	To read words or phrases and match them to their English translation
Resources	Two different coloured marker pens or chalks

1. Before pupils arrive, write jumbled French words on the left-hand side of the board and the English equivalents on the right-hand side. Leave space around each word as shown below.

2. Divide the class into two teams. Give each team a different coloured marker pen or chalk.

3. Representatives from each team take turns to come to the front of the class to draw a line linking a pair of words (French place name + its English equivalent). They must not cross any existing line.

4. If they make a correct match without crossing any other lines, they score a point for their team. If the match is not correct, or if they cannot reach the word they want without

crossing another line, they do not score. The winning team is the one with the most points at the end of the game.

Useful phrases

Viens au tableau.	Come to the board [to a single pupil].
Relie un mot français avec l'équivalent en anglais.	Match a French word with its English equivalent.
Attention: ne traverse pas la ligne !	Be careful: don't cross the line!

Comments

- The example above practises places in town. You could play the same game with almost any other topics too.

- You could progress to using short phrases instead of single words.

- If you want to introduce a writing element, pupils could make up similar puzzles on a sheet of paper, to play with a partner.

 As an alternative, you could write up sentence halves for more able or older pupils to match.

Increase the challenge by playing the following variation. Write a series of questions and answers in jumbled order on the board, with spaces between them. Representatives from each team take turns to come to the board and draw a line linking a question with its answer. They must read both aloud as they do it. As above, they must not cross an existing line.

Notes

....

....

....

....

....

....

....

....

....

....

....

....

....

2 Snap/*Bataille*

Step by step

The traditional game of Snap (the French equivalent is called *Bataille*) can be adapted so that pupils have to match words and pictures.

Classroom management	Pairs or small groups
Skill	Reading
Aim	To read a word or phrase and match it to a picture
Resources	Sets of small picture cards + word/phrase cards made to match the picture cards

1. Prepare the sets of cards in advance, or get pupils to make their own (check that the pictures are clear and unambiguous if they do).

2. Give each pair or group a set of picture cards and matching word cards.
   Pupil A takes the picture cards and Pupil B the words or phrases. They hold these face down.

3. In pairs, pupils play in the traditional way, taking it in turn to turn over the top card from their pile and place it in a pile in the centre of the desk.

4. If the word that follows a picture is a correct match – for example, a drawing of a dog then the word '*chien*' – the first pupil to call '*Bataille*' wins all the cards in the centre pile and adds them to the bottom of their own pile, face down like the rest. The winner is the player holding all the cards when the others have run out of cards, or with the most cards when time is up.

Useful phrases

À tour de rôle, retournez les cartes.   Take turns to turn the cards over.

Quand le mot va avec l'image, dites   If the word matches the card, shout
« Bataille » !   'Bataille'!

Comments

- You may need to have an umpire in each group in case more than one pupil calls at the same time. Alternatively, you could ask pupils to slap their hand down on the top of the pile as they call.

Increase the challenge by penalising any pupil who calls '*Bataille*' incorrectly. She must give the top card from her pile to her partner (or to the player on her right).

3 Word snake/*Serpent de mots*

Step by step

1. On the board, write a series of words or phrases in a wavy line with no spaces between the letters. Draw a simple snake's head at the start. For example, if you are working on the topic of colours, you could write:

Classroom management	Whole class
Skill	Reading (and writing)
Aim	To identify words in a string of letters
Resources	None

2. Pupils must read the string of letters, puzzle out the individual words and write them down separately, e.g. *bleu, blanc, rouge, noir, jaune, vert, gris, rose* (blue, white, red, black, yellow, green, grey, pink). They could do this as a beat-the-clock activity if you want to add a competitive element.

Useful phrases

Regardez le serpent. Look at the snake.

Trouvez et écrivez les mots. Find the words and write them out.

Comments

- The example above practises reading individual words, but the puzzle works well with sentences too. For example: *jeporteunpantalongris = Je porte un pantalon gris* (I wear grey trousers).

- You can even run two or three simple sentences together for older or more able classes. Encourage them to use capital letters and full stops where appropriate. For example:

jem'appelleMaxj'aionzeansjeportedesbaskets = Je m'appelle Max. J'ai onze ans. Je porte des baskets (My name is Max. I'm eleven years old. I'm wearing trainers).

Increase the challenge by replacing one or two letters with an asterisk and asking pupils to work out which letter it represents, e.g.

tuaim*slav*st*noir* = Tu aimes la veste noire ? (Do you like the black jacket?)

* = e

4 Find the pairs/*Trouvez les paires*

Step by step

1. Prepare the sets of cards in advance, or get pupils to make their own (check that the pictures are clear and unambiguous if they do).

2. Give each pair or group a set of picture cards and matching word cards.

3. The cards are turned over and shuffled, then placed face down in rows on the desk (or fixed to the board with adhesive tack if playing as a whole class).

4. Pupils take it in turn to turn over two cards, saying the appropriate word or phrase aloud as they do so. If they have a matching picture and word/phrase card, they keep the pair. If there is no match, the two cards are turned face down again, in the same position.

5. The game continues until all the pairs are matched. As pupils remember where the cards are, they are more likely to match a pair. The winner is the player with the most cards at the end of the game.

Classroom management	Whole class, small groups or pairs
Skill	Reading (also speaking, listening and observation and memory skills)
Aim	To practise reading to match words and pictures
Resources	A series of small picture cards or flashcards Word/phrase cards made to match the picture cards Adhesive tack

Useful phrases

C'est à moi !	It's my turn!
C'est à toi !	It's your turn!
C'est une paire.	It's a pair.
Bravo !	Well done!

Comments

- Make the cards in advance using clipart pictures or very simple drawings. The game is suitable for a variety of topics.

Increase the level of challenge by asking pupils to make up a sentence containing the word or phrase they have matched in order to win the cards.

For example: if a pupil has *Il fait beau* (the weather's nice) cards, he might say: *Quand il fait beau, je vais au jardin public* (When the weather's nice, I go to the park).

5   What's the word?/*À demi-mots*

Step by step

1. Before the lesson, take ten sheets of A4 paper and on each one write a word (or simple phrase) in large letters. Number these 1–10. For example, if you are learning the names of different European countries, you could write:

   1 *la France* (France), 2 *la Grande-Bretagne* (Great Britain), 3 *l'Irlande* (Ireland), 4 *l'Italie* (Italy), 5 *la Grèce* (Greece), 6 *l'Espagne* (Spain), 7 *la Belgique* (Belgium), 8 *la Pologne* (Poland), 9 *l'Allemagne* (Germany), 10 *la Suisse* (Switzerland).

Classroom management	Whole class
Skill	Reading
Aim	To read to decipher words
Resources	A4 sheets of paper Scissors for teacher Adhesive tack or drawing pins

2. Cut each one in half horizontally through the word. Put to one side the bottom part of each word.

3. Take the top halves, where only the top part of each letter is visible, and pin these up around the room.

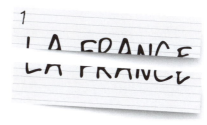

4. When pupils arrive, they must walk around the room trying to work out the word or phrase and write them out properly.

5. When everyone has finished, hand out the bottom halves to volunteers to pin up in the right places so that pupils can check their answers.

6. The winner is the child with the most correct answers.

Useful phrases

J'ai coupé les mots en deux parties.	I cut the words into two parts.
Faites le tour de la classe et lisez.	Go round the class and read.
Notez (le nom des pays de 1 à 10).	Make a note of (the countries from 1 to 10).

Comments

- At the end, offer bonus points if pupils can give the English equivalents of the words on their list.

Increase the challenge by setting a time limit.

6 Fish and chips/*Partenaires*

Step by step

1. Before the lesson, prepare a pad of sticky notes. Write a different word or phrase on each one. These should all be words pupils know well and that you want them to revise. Choose your words carefully so that they work in pairs.

Classroom management	Whole class
Skill	Reading
Aim	To read to find a word/phrase in a certain category
Resources	Pad of sticky notes

For example:

1 *la France* (France), 2 *la Grande-Bretagne* (Great Britain)

3 *Bonjour* (Hello), 4 *Au revoir* (Goodbye)

5 *lundi* (Monday), 6 *mardi* (Tuesday)

7 *janvier* (January), 8 *juin* (June)

9 *bleu* (blue), 10 *vert* (green)

11 *les mains* (hands), 12 *les pieds* (feet) etc.

2. At the start of the lesson, go round the class sticking a note on each pupil's forehead (or back). Be sure to let them see what it says first and if they are not sure what it means, tell them.

3. Pupils walk around the room reading each other's notes until they find their partner. The pair then comes to you to explain why they think they are partners, e.g. because they are both days of the week/colours/parts of the body.

4. The winning pair can then help you say whether the remaining pupils have found the right partners.

Useful phrases	*Lisez les mots.*	Read the words.
	Trouvez votre mot-partenaire.	Find your partner word.

Comments

- You could use a stopwatch to time how long it takes for all the pairs to team up. Can they beat that time when they play again next lesson?
- As a variation, have one word or phrase that does not have a partner. How quickly can the class decide who is the odd one out?

Increase the challenge by writing questions and answers for pupils to match.

Notes

7 Dominoes/*Les dominos*

Step by step

1. Make sets of picture dominoes in advance from stiff card (or get pupils to make their own sets). Draw or stick a simple picture on the left-hand side and write a word or short phrase on the right-hand side. Remember to start the sequence with a blank on the left-hand side of the first domino, and to finish with a blank on the right-hand side of the last one.

Classroom management	Small groups
Skill	Reading
Aim	To read and match words or short phrases to pictures
Resources	Home-made dominoes

For example, if you are working on telling the time, you might start:

2. Give a set of dominoes to each group. Pupils share them out equally.

3. The first player puts down any domino in the middle of the table.

4. The next player can add one of his dominoes to the left or the right of it if he has a word or picture that matches. If he can't go, he knocks on the table and play passes to the next player in the group.

5. The game continues until one player has laid all his dominoes. He is the winner.

Useful phrases

Trouvez le mot/la phrase qui va avec l'image.

Ajoutez un domino.

Find the word/sentence that goes with the picture.

Add a domino.

Comments

- Encourage pupils to use simple French phrases as they play, e.g.

  C'est à toi. (It's your go.)

Je passe. (I pass.)

Dépêche-toi ! (Hurry up!) etc.

 Increase the linguistic challenge by making the dominoes with sentence halves rather than words and pictures.

Notes

....

....

....

....

....

....

....

....

....

....

....

....

....

....

....

....

8 Sort it out/*Le tri*

Step by step

1. Before pupils arrive, write lots of words on the board, jumbled in random order. These words will be from two or more different groups, e.g. colours, days of the week, numbers, etc.

    For example:

Classroom management	Pairs, individuals or whole class
Skill	Reading
Aim	To read, understand and sort words into categories
Resources	Optional (if playing as a whole class): different coloured markers to write on the board Paper Coloured pens

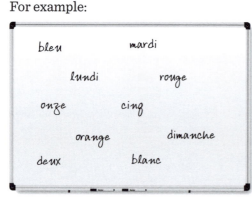

2. Pupils work individually or in pairs to sort the words into their different categories. They can write them in columns on a piece of paper (or, if you want to play as a whole class, you could allocate a different colour of pen to each category, e.g. blue for colours, red for days of the week). Pupils take turns to come to the front and circle one of the words in the right colour.

3. The winners are the pupils who sort all the words correctly in the shortest time. Alternatively, you can play as a class v. teacher game: if all the class finish before a certain time limit is reached, they have beaten you.

> **Useful phrases**
>
> *Regardez les mots.* Look at the words.
>
> *Quels mots vont ensemble ?* Which words go together?
>
> *Il faut trier le plus vite possible.* You have to sort as quickly as possible.

Comments

*   Once the sorting activity has been done, you could use the jumbled words again for a reading version of Kim's game (see page 63). Ask pupils to close their eyes. Rub out two or three of the words. When they open their eyes again, can they remember which words are missing?

Increase the challenge by including more categories and/or by including an odd word that doesn't belong to any of the categories and which pupils need to identify.

Notes

9 Good morning, postman/ *Bonjour, monsieur le facteur*

Step by step

1. Before the lesson, take six small pieces of paper and write a number (*un–six*) on each. Put each one into an envelope.

2. Before the class arrives, write six simple instructions on the board and number them.

Classroom management	Whole class
Skill	Reading
Aim	To read and react to an instruction
Resources	Six envelopes and six small pieces of paper

   For example, if you want to practise parts of the body, you might write:

   1 *Touchez-vous le nez (les pieds, l'oreille, etc.)* (Touch your nose (feet, ear, etc.)).

   2 *Dites oui avec la tête* (Nod your head).

   3 *Fermez les yeux* (Shut your eyes).

   4 *Levez la main* (Put up your hand).

   5 *Posez un crayon sur votre tête* (Put a pencil on your head).

   6 *Montrez-moi trois doigts* (Show me three fingers).

3. When the class arrives, choose a volunteer to be the 'postman'. Divide the rest of the class into six groups of three or four.

4. Write the name of a class member on the front of each envelope, making sure you have chosen at least one person from each group.

5. Explain that the postman (or woman) is going to deliver your letters. Hand him/her the envelopes.

6. The postman takes the first envelope to the child it is addressed to, saying: *Bonjour ! J'ai une lettre pour toi* (Hello! I have a letter for you).

7. The pupil takes the envelope on behalf of his group – not forgetting to say thank you to the postman – and opens the envelope.

8. In silence, the group reads the number on their piece of paper, finds the corresponding instruction on the board, and follows the instruction. For example, if they have *deux* on their piece of paper, they all start to nod their heads.

9. The rest of the class watches and works out which number was in the envelope by finding the instruction on the board that matches the action. They write it down in silence. Go round and check the answers and award a point for each correct number.

10. The postman delivers the next envelope and the process is repeated until all the letters are delivered.

11. Add up the points at the end. The team with the most points wins.

Tu es le facteur.	You are the postman [to a single pupil].
Distribue les lettres.	Deliver the letters [to a single pupil].
Ouvrez l'enveloppe.	Open the envelope.
Lisez l'instruction en silence.	Read the instruction in silence.
C'est quel numéro ?	What number is it?

Comments

- The example above practises parts of the body, but you could play the same game with the names of objects found in the classroom too.

  For example:

  1. *Montrez-moi deux crayons* (Show me two pencils).
  2. *Posez un livre sur vos genoux* (Put a book on your lap).
  3. *Mettez votre trousse dans votre cartable* (Put your pencil case into your school bag).
  4. *Touchez votre chaise* (Touch your chair).
  5. *Regardez par la fenêtre* (Look out of the window).
  6. *Montrez-moi un stylo* (Show me a pen).

Increase the challenge by including more instructions, or by making the instruction more complex, e.g. *Touchez trois fois le pied gauche avec la main droite* (Tap your left foot with your right hand three times).

Notes

....

....

....

....

....

....

10 Silly sentences/*Les phrases farfelues*

Step by step

1. Before pupils arrive, write words or phrases on the board in three or four columns, with each numbered 1–6. The words/phrases need to be such that choosing any element from each column will make up a grammatically correct sentence when read from left to right.

Classroom management	Small groups
Skill	Reading and speaking
Aim	To read sentences to see whether or not they make sense
Resources	Dice (one per group)

For example, if you are working on the topic of holidays:

	1st throw	2nd throw	3rd throw
1	*Un astronaute*	*va au bord de la mer*	*à bicyclette*
2	*Une princesse*	*va à la campagne*	*en avion*
3	*Un monstre*	*va à la montagne*	*et nage dans la mer*
4	*Un éléphant*	*reste à la maison*	*et fait du ski*
5	*Un garçon*	*va dans la jungle*	*et mange une glace*
6	*Une fille*	*va dans le désert*	*avec son chien*

2. Pupils play in groups of three or four. They take turns to roll a die three times and read out the phrases from the board that correspond to their throws. If they roll a 1, they read out '*Un astronaute*'. If they then throw a 3, they read out '*va à la montagne*' and so on. For example:

P1 (throws a 4, then a 6, then a 3): *Un éléphant va dans le désert et nage dans la mer* (An elephant goes to the desert and swims in the sea).

3. The group reads the sentence and decides whether or not it makes sense. If it does, the player scores a point. If the sentence is impossible or silly, then there is no score.

4. Once all the players have had three or four goes, the winner is the one with the most points.

Lancez le dé (trois fois).	Throw the die (three times).
Lisez la bonne ligne dans chaque colonne.	Read the right line in each column.
La phrase est bonne ou un peu farfelue ?	Is the sentence correct or a bit silly?

Comments

- For writing practice, pupils could write out their sentences and then illustrate them.
- For speaking practice, they could choose an element from each column to make a sentence which they then illustrate without writing a caption. Pupils can swap their finished drawings with a partner and see if their partner can say what is happening in each, using the words from the board.
- As a variation, you could make this a class v. teacher game. You secretly choose one element from each column and write your sentence on a piece of paper. Pupils must then guess what you have written by reading out various possibilities. If they can do it in under six guesses, they win. If they take more than that, you win.

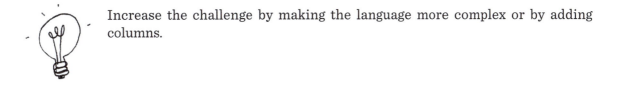 Increase the challenge by making the language more complex or by adding columns.

Notes

....

....

....

....

....

....

....

....

....

....

....

11 Mr Potato/*Monsieur Pomme de Terre*

Step by step

1. Draw on the board a potato-head character similar to this:

Classroom management	Individuals
Skill	Reading
Aim	To read a description of a person
Resources	Paper Coloured pens or pencils

2. Provide pupils with a checklist like the one below (either make photocopies to hand out or ask them to copy it from the board).

	oui	non
Il/Elle a		
les cheveux longs	❐	❐
les cheveux courts	❐	❐
un grand nez	❐	❐
un petit nez	❐	❐
des lunettes	❐	❐
une moustache	❐	❐
une barbe	❐	❐
un chapeau	❐	❐
etc.		

(He/She has long hair, short hair, a big nose, a small nose, glasses, a moustache, a beard, a hat)

3. Pupils read the checklist and tick the appropriate boxes to give a description of the character you have drawn.

4. Once they have finished, ask them to find a partner and compare their lists, helping each other (this is particularly effective if there is an incentive at the end; see Comments below).

5. Check your answers with the class.

Regardez Monsieur Pomme de Terre.   Look at Mr Potato.
Lisez et cochez la liste.   Read and tick the list.

Comments

- To make this activity into more of a game, offer an incentive for the class if everyone (or, with less able groups, maybe more than 80 per cent of the class) gets their checklist correct. The actual incentive will depend on your group and your circumstances (but could include their choice of a song to sing at the end of the lesson, a sweet, house points, etc.).

- Pupils could draw their own potato-head and then take a different coloured pen and tick the list again to build a description of it.

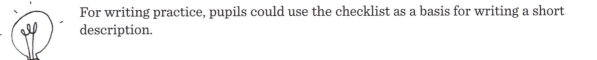

For writing practice, pupils could use the checklist as a basis for writing a short description.

Notes

....

....

....

....

....

....

....

....

....

....

....

....

12 3, 2, 1/ *Trois, deux, un*

Step by step

1. Before the lesson, prepare three sentences, each containing a key word.

   For example:

   La banane est un fruit
   (The banana is a fruit)

   Une banane est longue et jaune
   (A banana is long and yellow)

   Les singes aiment manger les bananes
   (Monkeys like eating bananas)

Classroom management	Whole class, in groups
Skill	Reading
Aim	To read a text and work out missing words
Resources	Paper Pens

2. Divide the class into teams of four or five pupils. The aim of the game is to guess the word that is missing from each sentence you write on the board. Each group chooses a team leader who will write their guesses.

3. Write your first sentence on the board, with a dotted line replacing the key word, e.g.

   La .... est un fruit.

4. The teams discuss what the missing word might be. When they have decided, the team leader writes their guess on a piece of paper and waves it in the air. You check the guesses, answering '*Oui*' or '*Non*'. Neither you nor the pupils call out the word. If the answer is correct, the team scores three points. If they are wrong, they wait for the next clue.

5. Write your second sentence on the board, e.g.

   Une .... est longue et jaune.

6. The teams who did not guess correctly the first time discuss what the missing word might be. You check their guesses as above. This time, a correct answer scores two points. If the guess is wrong, the team waits for the final clue.

7. Write your third sentence on the board, e.g.

   Les singes aiment manger les ....

8. The teams who still have not found the answer discuss what the missing word might be and you check their guesses. This time, a correct answer scores one point. If the guess is wrong, the team does not score.

9. Keep a note of each team's score. If you have prepared sentences with different key words, proceed as above with those. The winners are the team with the most points at the end of the activity.

Lisez la phrase.	Read the sentence.
Pour (trois/deux/un) point(s),	For (three/two/one) point(s),
devinez le mot qui manque.	guess the word that is missing.
Oui, c'est exact.	Yes, that's right.
Non, ce n'est pas ça.	No, it's not that.

Comments

- Explain at the start that the name of the game refers to the number of points pupils can score: three if they guess after seeing the first sentence, two after seeing the second sentence and one if they need to see all three sentences before a correct guess.
- This game is particularly good for cross-curricular work or Content and Language Integrated Learning (CLIL) activities. It tests pupils' general knowledge as well as their French.

For older/more able pupils, increase the challenge by using longer, more complex sentences, such as:

La .... *est un fruit riche en vitamine B qui est très bon pour la santé*

(The ....is a fruit rich in vitamin B which is very good for you).

Notes

....

....

....

....

....

....

....

....

....

....

13 The extra word/*Le mot en trop*

Step by step

1. Either on the board or on a photocopied sheet, provide pupils with a list of sentences, each of which contain a word that should not be there (a different word each time). For example, if you are working on the topic of what the children do in their spare time, you might write:

Classroom management	Pair-work
Skill	Reading
Aim	To read in order to spot the word which does not fit in a sentence
Resources	List of prepared sentences

1 *Le soir, je aller regarde la télé* (In the evening, I watch TV).

2 *J'aime beaucoup je écouter de la musique* (I like listening to music a lot).

3 *Je joue sur ma console avec mon frère préfère* (I play on my games console with my brother).

4 *Je n'aime pas jouer au cinéma football* (I don't like playing football).

5 *J'adore jouer du au piano* (I love playing the piano).

(NB: For your reference only, the grey highlighted words are the extra ones.)

2. Pupils work together in pairs, reading each sentence and deciding which is the extra word in each.

3. You could set a time limit and make this a beat-the-clock game.

Useful phrases

Lisez les phrases.	Read the sentences.
Dans chaque phrase, il y a un mot en trop.	In each sentence, there is one extra word.
Trouvez et notez le mot en trop.	Find and note down the extra word.

Comments

- For writing practice, pupils could make up similar sentences to swap with a partner. They could copy sentences from a course book or story book, adding their own extra words.

Increase the challenge by choosing the extra words so that, rearranged, they form a sentence of their own which pupils have to work out. For example, the highlighted words from the sentences above can be rearranged to make: *Je préfère aller au cinéma* (I prefer going to the cinema). Ask pupils to make a note of the extra words as they go along. Once they have them all, they put them in order to make a new sentence. The winning pair is the first to write out this sentence.

14 Lucky dip/*Le sac aux questions*

Step by step

1. In advance, write a number of questions on small cards (one per card) relating to the topic you are working on and/or others that you wish to revise. For example, if you are working on greetings and personal information, you might have:

   Ça va ? (How are you?)

   Comment tu t'appelles ? (What's your name?)

   Tu as quel âge ? (How old are you?)

   C'est quand, ton anniversaire ? (When is your birthday?)

   Tu habites où ? (Where do you live?)

   Tu as un animal à la maison ? (Have you got a pet?)

   Est-ce que tu aimes les chiens ? (Do you like dogs?)

   Tu as des frères et sœurs ? (Have you got any brothers and sisters?)

   C'est quoi, ta couleur préférée ? (What is your favourite colour?)

   C'est quoi, ton sport préféré ? (What is your favourite sport?)

   Put all the cards into your bag (or box).

2. Before pupils arrive, write on the board (numbered) answers to all but two or three of the questions. For example, for the questions above you might write seven of the following:

   1 *Ça va bien, merci !* (I'm fine, thanks.)

   2 *Je m'appelle Lili Leblanc.* (My name is Lili Leblanc.)

   3 *J'ai onze ans.* (I'm eleven.)

   4 *C'est en février.* (It's in February.)

   5 *J'habite à Paris.* (I live in Paris.)

   6 *J'ai un chat.* (I've got a cat.)

   7 *J'adore les chiens.* (I love dogs.)

   8 *J'ai deux frères.* (I've got two brothers.)

   9 *C'est le rouge.* (It's red.)

   10 *C'est le judo.* (It's judo.)

Classroom management	Whole class
Skill	Reading
Aim	To read a question and match it with an answer
Resources	A bag (or box) Cards with questions written on

3. Divide the class into two teams. The teams take turns to send a representative to the front of the class to dip into the bag and choose a card. They read the question aloud to the class. (You can help them with this if necessary.)

4. The rest of the team then has to find the correct answer from among those on the board. If they are correct, they keep the card. If they are wrong, they put the card back into the bag. If the answer to their question is not on the board, the card is put to one side.

5. The winning team is the one with the most cards once the bag is empty.

Prends une carte.	Take a card [to a single pupil].
Lis la question.	Read out the question [to a single pupil].
Vous pouvez trouver la bonne réponse au tableau ?	Can you find the right answer on the board?

Comments

- To avoid arguments or too much noise when deciding which answer is correct, you could ask pupils to vote with a show of hands.

Increase the challenge by introducing some answers that do not match exactly the questions in the bag. For example, to go with the questions above, you might write:

Elle s'appelle Lola. (Her name is Lola.)

Je déteste la gymnastique. (I hate gymnastics.)

Notes

....

....

....

....

....

....

....

....

15 Quiz time!/*À vos quiz !*

Step by step

Classroom management	Whole class, in pairs or individually
Skill	Reading
Aim	To read in order to do a quiz
Resources	None

1. Before pupils arrive, write a multiple-choice quiz on the board. For example, if you are working on the topic of family, you could include logic questions like these:

    (1) *Le père de ma mère, c'est ...* (My mother's father is)

        A *mon oncle* (my uncle)

        B *mon grand-père* (my grandfather)

        C *mon frère* (my brother)

    (2) *Le sœur de ma mère, c'est ...* (My mother's sister is)

        A *ma tante* (my aunt)

        B *ma grand-mère* (my grandmother)

        C *ma cousine* (my cousin)

    (3) *Le fils de mon oncle, c'est ...* (My uncle's son is)

        A *mon frère* (my brother)

        B *mon grand-père* (my grandfather)

        C *mon cousin* (my cousin)

2. Pupils read the text and answer the questions, either individually or in pairs.

3. Check answers. The highest score wins.

Useful phrases

Lisez les questions/les phrases. Read the questions/the sentences.

Notez vos réponses: A, B ou C. Make a note of your answers: A, B or C.

Comments

- Pupils generally enjoy logic questions like the ones above. You can easily adapt the idea for other topics. For food, for example, you could say:

    Faites avec des pommes de terre. Qu'est-ce que c'est ? (Made from potatoes. What is it?)

    A *une omelette* (an omelette)

    B *des frites* (chips)

    C *du fromage* (cheese)

Or for animals, you could say:

Je suis énorme et j'ai un très, très long nez. Qui suis-je ? (I am enormous and I have a very, very long nose. Who am I?)

A *une souris* (a mouse)

B *un lion* (a lion)

C *un éléphant* (an elephant)

- To focus on accurate spelling, you could provide alternative spellings of key words, e.g.

    Je suis un fruit rouge (I am a red fruit)

    A *une fraise* (a strawberry)

    B *une frais*

    C *une frèze*

- You could also use general knowledge questions.

- For writing practice, ask more able/older pupils to invent more questions to add to the quiz.

 Increase the challenge by setting a time limit. If you do this, discourage random guesses by deducting a point for each wrong answer when you check the answers.

Notes

....

....

....

....

....

....

....

....

....

16 Readalong/*Grand balayage*

Step by step

Classroom management	Whole class
Skill	Reading
Aim	To read and listen to reinforce sound–spelling links
Resources	Text

1. Give each pupil a copy of a text. You could use a text from a course book or story book, or you could make up a text of your own. It does not matter if pupils don't know all the words in the text, but they should be able to recognise some. For example, for beginners, if you are working on the topic of sport, you might use the following:

   Jade adore le sport. (Jade loves sport.)

   Son sport préféré, c'est le ski. En février, elle fait du ski dans les Alpes. Elle est très forte. (Her favourite sport is skiing. In February, she goes skiing in the Alps. She is very good at it.)

   En été, quand il fait beau, elle va au centre sportif et elle joue au football avec ses amies. (In the summer, when the weather is nice, she goes to the sports centre and plays football with her friends.)

   La mère de Jade joue souvent au tennis le dimanche matin. (Jade's mother often plays tennis on Sunday mornings.)

   Son père préfère jouer au golf. (Her father prefers to play golf.)

2. Divide the class into two teams. Ideally, they should sit on different sides of the room.

3. Tell pupils that you are going to read the text aloud. They must read along with you, following the words of the text but not speaking. At some point, you will stop and pupils must call out the word that comes next. For example, using the text above:

   T: *Jade adore le sport. Son ...*

   Pupils: *sport*

4. The team that calls out the correct word first scores a point. Deduct a point for wrong calls.

5. If you come to the end of the text, you can start again at the beginning, stopping at different places this time.

Useful phrases

Écoutez et suivez le texte.	Listen and follow the text.
Quand je m'arrête, dites le mot suivant.	When I stop, say the following word.
Bravo, un point pour l'équipe rouge.	Well done, a point to the red team.

Comments

- It is much better if you have enough copies of a text for each pupil to have their own, but if this is not possible, you could write a text on the board in advance. Ensure the writing is large enough for all to see clearly.

- The length of text will vary depending on the level of the class. For beginners, it should be several sentences long, but for older or more able groups, several paragraphs will be more effective.

- If the class all call out so quickly that it is hard to tell who was first, you could nominate just two pupils from each team to call out each time.

- Once the game is finished, ask comprehension questions in French or in English to check how much of the text pupils can understand. For example, *Qui fait du ski ?* (Who goes skiing?), *Quel sport aime sa mère ?* (What sport does her mum like?), and so on.

 If the text is familiar, more able pupils could play in small groups, with a pupil reading the text aloud.

Notes

....

....

....

....

....

....

....

....

....

17 Build a song/*Construisez une chanson*

Step by step

1. Before the lesson, choose a song or poem pupils know well. Write each line on a separate card or sheet of paper. These will be the 'bricks' pupils use to build the song. If you can make them look a bit like bricks, all the better!

Classroom management	Groups
Skill	Reading
Aim	To read and arrange song lyrics in the correct order
Resources	Cards with lines of song or poem written on

2. Give each brick to a pupil to hold and read. If there are ten lines in the song, as there are in the winter song here, there should be a group of ten pupils.

   Vive le vent

   Vive le vent

   Vive le vent d'hiver

   Qui s'en va sifflant soufflant

   Dans les grands sapins verts

   Oh ! Vive le temps

   Vive le temps

   Vive le temps d'hiver

   Boule de neige et jour de l'an

   Et bonne année grand-mère

   > Vive le vent

3. This is a beat-the-clock game. On a signal from you, all the pupils with a card come together at the front of the class. The aim is for them to read each other's sentences and form a line with the lyrics in the correct order, if the class reads from left to right.

4. The rest of the class can help them get into the right positions by reading the cards and shouting out their names and the words '*À droite !*' (Right!) or '*À gauche !*' (Left!).

5. Time how long it takes the group to 'build' the song in the right order. Then all sing the song together, reading the lyrics from left to right, to make sure the order works.

6. Challenge another group to beat that time, either with the same or a different song.

Useful phrases		
Voici une brique.		Here's a brick.
Lisez les phrases.		Read the sentences.
Mettez les lignes de la chanson dans le bon ordre.		Put the lines of the song in the right order.

Comments

• You could challenge the group to beat their own time in a subsequent lesson.

Increase the challenge by holding back one of the bricks. Give the group a blank card instead. Pupils have to work out which line of the song is missing and write it on the blank card. They can then complete the song as before. Check whether they have written the missing line correctly by comparing it with the card you kept back.

Notes

....

....

....

....

....

....

....

....

....

....

....

18 Invisible words/*Les mots invisibles*

Step by step

Classroom management	Whole class
Skill	Reading
Aim	To read and re-create a text
Resources	Text

1. Before pupils arrive, write a text on the board, starting a new line for each sentence. This might be a text from a course book or story book, or you could make up a text of your own. Songs and poems work particularly well. Choose a text with language pupils are familiar with. The text should not be too long; one verse of a song should be enough. For example:

    J'ai de la confiture (I have jam), *sur toute la figure* (all over my face), *et du chocolat* (and chocolate), *du haut jusqu'en bas* (from top to bottom), *Une moustache de chat* (a cat's moustache/whiskers), *Ah là là là !* (Oh dear!)

2. When pupils arrive, ask them to skim-read the text in silence. If there are any words they don't understand, help them out.

3. The whole class then reads the text aloud, as a chorus. Read along with them.

4. Now rub out one of the words – let pupils see which one it is. Replace it with dashes.

    For example:

    Une＿＿＿＿＿＿＿＿de chat

5. Pupils read the whole text aloud again. They have to say the missing – or invisible – word, from memory, so that the poem is still complete orally.

6. Repeat steps 4 and 5 several times, each time rubbing out a new word, until at the end pupils are 'reading' the whole rhyme from the 'invisible' words, i.e. from memory.

> **Useful phrases**
>
> *Lisons tous ensemble.* Let's all read together.
> *Ce mot est invisible maintenant.* That word is invisible now.
> *Lisons encore une fois.* Let's read it again.

Comments

*   To simplify the activity, leave in the first letter each time you rub out a word.
*   You could ask a pupil to suggest which word to rub out next.

 Increase the challenge by choosing longer or more complex texts.

19 Eagle eye/*L'œil de lynx*

Step by step

1. Give each pupil a copy of a text. This might be a text from a course book or story book, or you could make up a text of your own. It doesn't matter if pupils don't understand all the words in the text, but they should be able to recognise some. Tell them to turn the text over so it's face down in front of them.

Classroom management	Individual or pairs
Skill	Reading
Aim	To scan a longer text to find a specific piece of information
Resources	Longish text

2. Set pupils a task. For example, one of the following:
   - read the text and note down the longest word
   - note all the five-letter words
   - note all the words that are the same (or almost) as English (known as 'cognates' or *mots transparents*)
   - make a note of all the nouns (or verbs, or adjectives).

3. On your signal, pupils turn over the text and scan it, looking for the word(s) to complete the task.

4. The first pupil to find the correct word(s) is the winner.

Useful phrases

Cherchez (le mot le plus long/ tous les mots de cinq lettres). Find (the longest word/all the five-letter words).

À vos marques, prêts, partez ! On your marks, get set, go!

Comments

- You could make a large cardboard 'eye' badge to award the winner.
- Once the task is completed, ask comprehension questions in French or in English to see how much of the text pupils can understand.

Increase the challenge by writing on the board two or more tasks for pupils to complete once they have finished the first. That way, they will have to reread the text several times.

20 The missing sentence/*La phrase qui manque*

Step by step

1. Prepare the six dialogues, using language with which pupils are already familiar. For example, for a shopping dialogue:

   You could vary the dialogue for the remaining groups by substituting the names of different items of food to buy at different market stalls: *un melon* (a melon) or *des pommes* (apples) at the fruit stall; *une tarte aux fraises* (a strawberry tart) or *deux éclairs au chocolat* (two chocolate éclairs) at the *pâtisserie* (bakery) stall, etc.

2. Choose seven pupils to be 'callers' and then divide the rest of the class into six pairs or groups.

Classroom management	Whole class: seven callers and the rest of the class divided into six groups
Skill	Reading, speaking, listening and writing
Aim	To revise short dialogues
Resources	Prepare in advance six similar dialogues, cut into strips, plus one extra strip with a sentence that does not fit in any of the dialogues. See the example below
	Store the strips for each dialogue in different envelopes

Bonjour. Vous désirez ?

Bonjour. Je voudrais une baguette, s'il vous plaît.

Voilà. C'est tout ?

Non, vous avez aussi des croissants ?

Ah non, désolé. Je n'ai pas de croissants aujourd'hui. J'ai des pains au chocolat.

D'accord, deux pains au chocolat, s'il vous plaît.

Ça fait quatre euros vingt, s'il vous plaît.

Vous voulez aller au cinéma ce soir ?

3. From each of your six prepared envelopes, remove one strip at random. Give each of the callers a strip. Give the seventh caller the odd strip. Don't let the rest of the class see who has what.

4. The aim of the activity is to make a complete dialogue. Tell the groups that in their envelope they have strips of paper which they must put in the correct order to make up a dialogue. However, there is one sentence/strip missing. They will have a few minutes to read the sentences, try to arrange them and identify where there might be a sentence missing. While the groups are working, the callers walk around the class, reading aloud the sentence on their strip.

5. When a group works out who is saying the sentence that fits with their dialogue, they grab the caller. Without looking at his strip, they listen carefully (the caller may need to repeat it several times) and write out the missing sentence on a piece of paper which they insert in the right place in their dialogue. The first team to finish is the winner.

Useful phrases		
Mettez les phrases dans le bon ordre.	Arrange the sentences in the right order.
Il y a une phrase qui manque.	There is one sentence missing.
Écoutez et trouvez la phrase qui vous manque.	Listen to find your missing sentence.

Comments

- Allow enough time for all the groups to complete their dialogues. They can then act them out for the class to check.

- Use language pupils are already familiar with. As well as shopping dialogues, you could have conversations ordering food and drink in a café or restaurant, or interviews finding out information such as age, birthday and hobbies.

You could increase the level of linguistic challenge by using the activity to focus on a point of grammar, such as gender and adjective agreement.

For example:

Ton frère est blond ? (Is your brother blond?)

Non, il est brun. (No, he has brown hair.)

Ta sœur aussi ? (Your sister as well?)

Non, elle est brune. (No, she has brown hair.)

For more advanced classes, increase the challenge by only giving each group the topic of a conversation; for example, *à la boulangerie* (at the baker's), *aux fruits et légumes* (at the greengrocer's), etc. Give out all the strips for the conversations, one to each pupil. They move around, saying their sentences aloud. Proceed as above until the different groups have come together with their sentences and all the dialogues have been re-created.

Part 4: Writing

There are a variety of ways that young learners can write in French. In the games we include here, they have the opportunity to progress from single words to texts of increasing length by:

- copying words and phrases
- listening and writing
- writing familiar words, phrases and sentences independently
- using a model or writing frame
- adapting and substituting words and phrases.

Some games from other parts of this book involve some writing, or can be adapted to include it, and these are listed below.

Part 1: Listening – games 8 and 11

Part 2: Speaking – games 11 and 12

Part 3: Reading – games 3 and 5

Part 5: Numbers – games 5, 11, 16–19

Part 6: Grammar – games 4, 9–11, 13, 15

Part 7: Playing with sounds – games 13, 19, 20.

1 Finger writing/*Au bout des doigts*

Step by step

1. Prepare in advance a list of vocabulary you want the pupils to practise. For example, for family members: *mon père* (my father), *ma mère* (my mother), *mon frère* (my brother), *ma sœur* (my sister), *mon beau-père* (my stepfather), *ma belle-mère* (my stepmother), *mon demi-frère* (my stepbrother), *mon cousin* (my cousin), etc.

Classroom management	Pair-work
Skill	Writing
Aim	To copy familiar words
Resources	Vocabulary list

2. Write the vocabulary list on the board.

3. Pupils play in pairs. Pupil 1 looks at the list, selects a word and writes it with his finger on the palm of Pupil 2's hand. There is no need to start at the top of the list.

4. If Pupil 2 guesses the word correctly, he scores a point. If Pupil 2 notices a spelling mistake, he corrects it and gets an extra point.

5. It's then Pupil 2's turn to pick a word and write it on his partner's hand. Repeat the process for all the words. The pupil with most points at the end of the game wins.

Useful phrases

Jouez à deux.

Choisis un mot au tableau.

Écris le mot avec le doigt dans la main de ton/ta partenaire.

Play in pairs.

Choose a word on the board [to a single pupil].

Write the word with your finger on your partner's hand.

Comments

- Make sure you have an odd number of words on the board, so that there are always at least two words for pupils to choose from. The game ends when there is only one word left on the board.

 To increase the level of challenge, ask pupils to come up with their own words related to the topic you're doing. They do not have models to copy, so they write them from memory on their partner's hand.

2   Back writing/*Sur le dos*

Step by step

1. Decide on the topic you want pupils to practise. For example, you could choose holidays. Write a list of related words on a piece of paper.

2. Divide the class into teams of up to eight. Each team lines up, facing the board. Give a board pen each to the pupils nearest the board.

Classroom management	Whole class/teams
Skill	Writing
Aim	To copy familiar words
Resources	List of words Board pens

3. Show a word from your list to the pupils at the back of each line. For example:

   la mer (sea), *la plage* (beach), *le sable* (sand), *le parasol* (sun umbrella), *la serviette* (towel), *le chapeau* (hat), etc. She then writes each letter of the word with her finger on the back of the pupil in front.

4. The word is then passed from one pupil to the next in the same way until it reaches the first pupil in the line, who rushes to write the word on the board and then runs to the back of the line. The first team with the word correctly spelled wins a point.

> **Useful phrases**
>
> *Mettez-vous en équipes.* Divide into teams.
>
> *Regarde/Écoute le mot.* Look at/Listen to the word.
>
> *Écris le mot avec ton doigt sur le dos de l'élève devant toi.* Write the word with your finger on the back of the person in front of you.

Comments

- With younger learners, use short words. You could also ask them to pass the word down the line one letter at a time.

 The more pupils in a line, the more difficult the task.

3   Bang!/*Bang !*

Step by step

Classroom management	Whole class/teams
Skill	Writing
Aim	To copy familiar words
Resources	Cards Non-transparent bag

1. Prepare in advance a number of cards (depending on the number of pupils in your class) with words/ phrases you want the class to practise. For example, to revise the names of musical instruments, write: *un piano* (piano), *un violon* (violin), *un violoncelle* (cello), *une flûte* (flute), *une trompette* (trumpet), *une harpe* (harp), *une guitare* (guitar), *une batterie* (drum kit), etc. Include a few cards with the word '*Bang !*'

2. Shuffle the cards and place them in a non-transparent bag.

3. Divide the class into two teams. Decide on a set time for the game.

4. Call a pupil from Team A to the board. Without peeking, she takes a card from the bag, looks at it and writes the word on the board.

5. Her teammates read the word and say whether they agree with the spelling. They can make suggestions which the pupil at the board can take or leave. If the word is spelled correctly, she keeps the card. If it's not spelled correctly, put the card back into the bag.

6. Next, call a player from Team B to the board and repeat the process. If a pupil takes a '*Bang !*' card, her team loses all their cards, which go back in the bag.

7. When time is up, the team with most cards wins.

Sors une carte du sac.	Take a card from the bag.
Écris le mot au tableau.	Write the word on the board.
Vous êtes tous d'accord ?	Do you all agree?

Comments

•   You could use this activity to revise vocabulary from a variety of topic areas or grammatical features.

•   For more advanced pupils, include cards with short phrases or sentences. For example, for the topic of music, you could include: *jouer du piano* (to play the piano), *jouer de la guitare* (to play the guitar), *elle joue de la flûte* (she plays the flute), *il ne joue pas d'instrument* (he doesn't play an instrument).

Vary the level of challenge by increasing or decreasing the level of support. For younger pupils, leave the word they have to spell in full view. Alternatively, cover up either the bottom half or top half of the word with a blank card. More advanced pupils can look at the word, turn the card over and write it from memory.

Notes

4   Beat the clock/*Contre la montre*

Step by step

1. Write or display on the board a selection of words which you want pupils to revise. For example, names of sports including '*faire de*':

   Je fais ... du judo (judo)

   de la natation (swimming)

   du basket (basketball)

   de l'équitation (horse-riding)

   du ski (skiing)

   de l'athlétisme (athletics)

   de la voile (sailing)

   de la danse classique (ballet)

   de la gymnastique (gymnastics).

Classroom management	Whole class
Skill	Writing
Aim	To copy familiar words
Resources	Vocabulary list Timer

2. Tell pupils they have one minute to look at the words very carefully.

3. Cover the words after the minute is up and set the timer. Pupils must write down as many words as they can remember.

4. Pupils get two points for each word remembered and spelled correctly, and one point if it is not correctly spelled.

Regardez bien les mots.	Look at the words carefully.
Vous avez une minute.	You have one minute.
Maintenant, écrivez les mots.	Now write down the words.

Useful phrases

Comments

- A variation is to read out a list of words two or three times to the class, pausing for a minute at the end of each reading. They listen carefully and write down as many words as they can remember. As above, they get two points for each word remembered and spelled correctly, and one point if it is not correctly spelled.

To make it more challenging, add more words and reduce the length of time pupils have to look at them.

To vary the level of challenge, give younger learners one word to write. How many times can they write that word correctly in one minute?

5 Dial a word/*La télélettre*

Step by step

1. Revise the topic/unit vocabulary before playing this game.

2. Prepare a list of topic-related words. For instance, if you want to revise school equipment, you could have:

   un sac (bag), *un stylo* (pen), *un livre* (book), *un crayon* (pencil), *une règle* (ruler), *un cahier* (exercise book), *une trousse* (pencil case), *une tablette* (tablet), etc.

   Encode each word using the dial pad.

   For example, *un sac* = 86 722.

3. In class, display the dial pad. Write the encoded words on the board, one at a time.

4. Individually or in pairs, pupils must crack the code and write out each word on a piece of paper or on their whiteboards, if they use them. They get a point per word correctly decoded and spelled. The winner is the pupil/the pair with the most points.

Classroom management	Whole class/Pair-work
Skill	Writing
Aim	To write a familiar word letter by letter
Resources	Vocabulary list Picture of a dial pad Optional: whiteboards and pens

Useful phrases

Trouvez le mot codé. Work out the coded word.

Comments

- Working in pairs, pupils could make up their own encoded words for the class (or another pair) to decode. Make sure they have spelled their words correctly before they exchange them or offer them to the class.

- A variation of this is to make and use a code wheel using coloured sections.

To increase the level of challenge, pupils could decode whole sentences.

For example:

2'378 62 8768773   5'24 86 722
C'est ma trousse.   *J'ai un sac.*

6 Pizza/*Pizza*

Step by step

This is a traditional game in which players work out a word by guessing its letters before the pizza disappears (one piece of pizza is removed each time they choose a wrong letter).

Classroom management	Whole class/teams
Skill	Writing
Aim	To write a familiar word, letter by letter
Resources	Vocabulary list Pens

1. Select the words you want pupils to practise; for example, parts of the face:

    les cheveux (hair)

    les yeux (eyes)

    le nez (nose)

    les joues (cheeks)

    la bouche (mouth)

    les dents (teeth)

    le menton (chin).

2. Pupils can play the game individually or you can divide the class into teams. First, revise the alphabet to make sure they can all say the letters.

3. Draw dashes on the board to indicate the number of letters contained in the mystery word. For example, for *cheveux*, draw: _ _ _ _ _ _ _.

4. Team A starts by suggesting a letter. If that letter is in the word, write it in the correct position. Team A has another go. If the letter they choose isn't in the word, erase one section from the pizza you have drawn on the board.

5. It is now Team B's turn to suggest a letter. Proceed as above.

6. Repeat with other words. The winning team is the one with the largest amount of pizza remaining.

Useful phrases

Dites une lettre.　　　　Say a letter.

Oui, il y a un X ici.　　　Yes, there's an X here.

Non, il n'y a pas de Y dans le mot.　　No, there's no Y in the word.

Comments

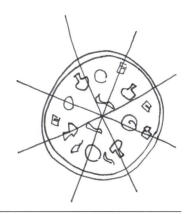

- Decide on the number of sections for your pizza; for example, cut the pizza into eight, twelve or more pieces.
- You could decide to choose a different image: for instance, a raft made of up to ten parts which you rub out one at a time with each wrong guess, leaving you stranded on a desert island, or a flower with up to ten petals and leaves, which also disappear with each wrong letter.

 You can increase the level of challenge by choosing random words.

For bonus points, once they've guessed it, ask pupils to pronounce the word, to give its meaning and to use it in a sentence.

Notes

7 Dice of fortune/*Les dés de la fortune*

Step by step

This is a variation on the pizza game using sentences rather than individual words. Make sure you revise the alphabet first so that all pupils can name letters.

Classroom management	Whole class/groups
Skill	Writing
Aim	To write sentences, letter by letter
Resources	Dice

1. Divide the class into groups. Give each group a die.

2. Write a Pizza-style blank sentence on the board. Make sure pupils are aware of the number of words involved by leaving big gaps between each word or numbering them.

3. Pupils roll the die before they name a letter from the alphabet.

4. Award points according to how many of their chosen letters appear in the puzzle. For example, if a pupil rolls a 3 and says 'e', her group would get three points for every 'e' found in the sentence.

   Add an element of luck: if she rolls a 1, the group loses all its points.

5. The group that works out the complete sentence gets a bonus point.

6. The group with most points wins.

Useful phrases

Mettez-vous en groupes.	Divide into groups.
Dites une lettre.	Say a letter.
Si la lettre est dans la phrase, vous gagnez des points.	If the letter is in the sentence, you win points.
Lancez le dé pour savoir combien de points.	Throw the die to find out how many points.
Si vous faites un 1, vous perdez tous vos points.	If you throw a 1, you lose all your points.

Comments

- You can choose sentences that relate to the topic you've just done in class, or you can make up sentences about any previously learned topic for revision purposes.

 To increase the level of challenge, increase the length of the sentences.

8   Letter by letter/*Une lettre à la fois*

Step by step

1. Prepare a vocabulary list on the topic you wish to revise. For example, for places in town:

   la piscine (swimming pool), *la biblio-thèque* (library), *le stade* (stadium), *le jardin public* (park), *la patinoire* (ice rink), *le musée* (museum).

Classroom management	Whole class/teams
Skill	Writing
Aim	To listen and write familiar words, letter by letter
Resources	Vocabulary list

2. Divide the class into two teams, who line up facing the board.

3. The first pupil from each team comes to the board. Call out the first word on your list. He writes the first letter of that word, passes the pen to the second pupil in his team and then goes to the end of the line.

4. Pupil 2 comes to the board and writes the second letter of the word, Pupil 3 the third letter, etc. until the whole word is written. If a pupil makes a mistake, he must erase the whole word and start again from the beginning. Repeat the process until the entire word is spelled correctly.

5. Repeat the process with a different word from your list.

6. The winning team is the first team to correctly spell all the words on your list.

Useful phrases

Écoutez le mot.	Listen to the word.
Écris la première/deuxième/troisième lettre.	Write the first/second/third letter [to a single pupil].
Tu as fait une faute.	You've made a mistake [to a single pupil].
Efface tout !	Rub everything out [to a single pupil]!

Comments

• The aim of the game (to practise spelling words one letter at a time) gives you an opportunity to reinforce the use of accents and highlight difficult sound–spelling links. For example, some sounds can be made up of several letters, such as 'in' is (i + n/m) or 'o' (a + u or e + a + u).

To increase the level of challenge, broaden the lexical field to include several topic areas.

For bonus points, you could also ask each team to pronounce the completed word correctly and to give its meaning in English.

9 Concertina spelling/*L'accordéon*

Step by step

This game is good for revising vocabulary at the end of a topic. For example, you could focus on vocabulary relating to Christmas: *le Père Noël* (Father Christmas), *le renne* (reindeer), *le traîneau* (sledge), *la cheminée* (chimney), *le cadeau* (present), *le sapin* (Christmas tree), *la guirlande* (tinsel), *la boule* (bauble), *la dinde* (turkey), *la bûche* (Christmas log), etc.

Classroom management	Whole class/groups
Skill	Writing
Aim	To listen to and write familiar words
Resources	Paper and pen

1. Give a sheet of paper and a pen to each group (five or six pupils).

2. Say a word aloud. The whole class listens carefully.

3. Pupil 1 writes the word at the top of the page before passing the sheet to Pupil 2.

4. Pupil 2 checks the word. If she agrees with the spelling, she writes it out again underneath. If she doesn't agree with the spelling, she writes it down differently underneath. Then she folds the paper in order to cover the first word, but leaves the second showing.

5. Pupil 2 passes the paper to Pupil 3 who checks, copies and folds – or checks, rewrites and folds – before passing it to Pupil 4. Continue this way until all members of the group have written the word.

6. At the end of a round, each team unfolds their paper and scores one point per word correctly spelled. The group with most points wins.

> **Useful phrases**
>
> | | |
> |---|---|
> | *Écoutez et écrivez.* | Listen and write. |
> | *Lisez le mot.* | Read the word. |
> | *Corrigez le mot.* | Correct the spelling of the word. |
> | *Pliez/dépliez le papier.* | Fold/unfold the paper. |

Comments

• A variation on this is Rounds: the first pupil in each group writes a word on the sheet and passes it on to Pupil 2, who must check the spelling and write a different word related to the topic (without folding the paper this time), before passing the sheet to Pupil 3 who does the same.

- After a given time, stop the game. Each word correctly spelled scores a point, and an extra point if it has not been mentioned by any other group.

 Increase the level of linguistic challenge by giving pupils longer phrases or sentences they are familiar with to copy. For example, *j'adore Noël* (I love Christmas), *on mange de la dinde* (we eat turkey), *on va chez mes grands-parents le jour de Noël* (we go to my grandparents on Christmas Day).

Notes

....

....

....

....

....

....

....

....

....

....

....

....

....

....

....

10 Puzzle it out!/*Casse-tête !*

Step by step

This is a matching game in the shape of a puzzle, based on the idea of tarsia puzzles which are often used in maths. It is ideal to check if pupils have understood the meaning of the French they have learned by asking them to match it to English.

Classroom management	Whole class/groups
Skill	Writing
Aim	To write from memory
Resources	Photocopied puzzle sheet (tarsia style) Scissors

1. Prepare a puzzle in advance. Start with simple shapes like the one below (with six or nine segments).

2. Write the English equivalent of the phrases you want pupils to revise. For example, for directions you could write:

   straight on (*tout droit*)

   to the right (*à droite*)

   to the left (*à gauche*)

   turn (*tournez*)

   go (*allez*)

   take (*prenez*)

   the first on the right (*la première à droite*)

   the second on the left (*la deuxième à gauche*).

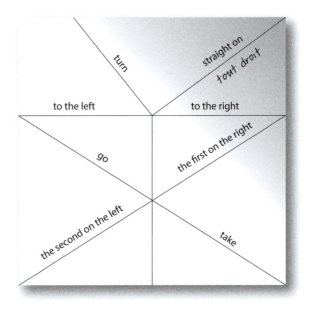

3. Photocopy and hand out the puzzle sheets, one per pupil or group of pupils.

4. Pupils complete the puzzle by writing in the corresponding French words/phrases underneath the English ones. Circulate to check they have written them correctly. The first pupil/group to finish wins a point.

5. Then pupils cut up the page into different segments and shuffle them. The first pupil/group to reassemble the puzzle wins an extra point.

Useful phrases

Complétez le puzzle en français.   Complete the puzzle in French.

Découpez les morceaux du puzzle.   Cut out the bits of the puzzle.

Reconstituez le puzzle.   Put the puzzle back together again.

Comments

- If you don't want to practise writing, this game can be a simple reading exercise: you write in both the French and English phrases, pupils cut up the pieces and match them up.

- The puzzle can also be adapted to matching questions to answers, positive and negative sentences, opposites, singular and plurals, etc. It is useful for revising numbers, time and grammar points.

- You can also hand out blank puzzle sheets, and pairs or groups make up their own puzzles for other groups to play with.

 To increase the level of challenge, increase the number of segments in the puzzle.

Notes

....

....

....

....

....

....

....

....

....

....

11 Writing by numbers/*Écrire par numéros*

Step by step

This game (inspired by painting by numbers) helps pupils make full sentences (short or extended) using a writing frame for support.

Classroom management	Whole class
Skill	Writing (and reading)
Aim	To introduce writing sentences using a writing frame
Resources	Writing frame (words or pictures)

1. Prepare a writing frame in advance, on a topic of your choice, such as food likes and dislikes (see below). Each square has a number. For example:

1 *J'adore*	5 *les gâteaux*	9 *et*	11 *j'adore*	15 *les œufs*
2 *J'aime bien*	6 *les fruits*	10 *mais*	12 *j'aime bien*	16 *les poires*
3 *Je n'aime pas*	7 *les légumes*		13 *je n'aime pas*	17 *les carottes*
4 *Je déteste*	8 *la viande*		14 *je déteste*	18 *le poisson*

2. Write or display the writing frame on the board.
3. Write a number sequence on the board, using one from each column.

   For example, write:

   1 6 10 13 16 (Answer: *J'adore les fruits mais je n'aime pas les poires* (I love fruit but I don't like pears).)

4. Pupils must find the numbers in the grid and copy the words to make the sentence.

5. The first ten pupils who have correctly written the sentence win a point.

6. Repeat several times with different numbers.

Useful phrases

Écoutez bien les numéros.	Listen carefully to the numbers.
Trouvez les numéros dans la grille.	Write the numbers in the frame.
Écrivez la phrase complète.	Write out the whole sentence.

Comments

- A variation of this game is to use symbols instead of words in the writing frame. For example:

- Ask pupils to come up with their own number sequences and the rest of the class to write down the sentences.

To increase the level of challenge, make more columns so that pupils can make longer sentences.

12 Race to the board/*La course au tableau*

Step by step

1. Divide the class into two or more teams, depending on the size of the class. Divide the board into sections, as many as you have teams.

2. Choose a topic that you want pupils to practise, for example sports.

3. Explain that each team has three minutes to come to the board to write

Classroom management	Whole class/teams
Skill	Writing
Aim	To write familiar words from memory
Resources	Different coloured pens

on their section of the board as many words as possible related to the topic. For example, they could write:

nager (to swim)   *jouer* (to play)   *la raquette* (racket)

le basket (basketball)   *le balle* (ball)   etc.

Tell pupils that the team must remain quiet at all times and nobody is allowed to help the pupil who is writing.

4. At a signal from you, one pupil from each team runs to the board and writes a word related to the topic. Each pupil only writes one word at a time, then rushes back to pass the pen to another member of their team, and so on. Do not correct any mistakes at this stage.

5. After three minutes, stop the race and count up the words. Give one point for each word relevant to the topic, add one point if it is spelled correctly and a bonus point if the word hasn't been used by any other groups. The group with most points wins.

> **Useful phrases**

Cours au tableau et écris un mot.	Run to the board and write a word [to a single pupil].
Passe le crayon à un autre élève de l'équipe.	Pass the pen to another team member [to a single pupil].
Comptons les mots.	Let's count the words.

Comments

- A variation of this, which can be done with the whole class remaining seated, is Word sun: draw a sun with at least six rays on the board. Choose a topic to be revised and write it in the centre of the sun. For example: *le sport*.

- Pupils copy the sun and write words related to the topic at the tip of each ray. Follow step 5 as above.

- Make it more demanding by adding more rays to the sun or ask pupils to write full sentences. For example: *Je vais nager à la piscine (le lundi).* (I go swimming at the swimming pool (on Mondays).)
- You could adapt this game to play with words containing certain sounds.

 To increase the challenge, ask pupils to read the words they have written, translate them and use them in a sentence.

Notes

....

....

....

....

....

....

....

....

....

....

....

....

....

....

....

13 Roll the dice/À vos dés

Step by step

1. Decide on a topic area you want pupils to practise/revise.

2. Throw one die (or two dice) and write the numbers shown on the board for the class to see.

Classroom management	Pair-work
Skill	Writing
Aim	To write words/sentences
Resources	Dice (giant size, ideally)

3. Pupils work in pairs. They write down a word or words that contains the number of letters indicated by the die. For example, if you're revising colours and they throw a 4, pupils could write: *rose* (pink), *vert* (green), *bleu* (blue), *noir* (black) or *gris* (grey).

4. Each pair scores one point for each word spelled correctly.

Useful phrases

Écrivez un mot de (cinq) lettres.   Write a (five)-letter word.

Comments

- A variation of this game for general revision of vocabulary is to choose a letter of the alphabet at random. The die then dictates the number of words pupils need to write that start with that letter.

  So if you select the letter F and throw a 5, pupils write five words starting with F; for example:

  famille (family)   *faim* (hunger)

  frère (brother)   *froid* (cold)

  français (French)

Increase the level of challenge by asking pupils to write a sentence with the number of words indicated by the die/dice. For example, if the die shows 5, on the theme of colour, pupils could write: *Il aime beaucoup le vert* (He likes green) or *Je mange des haricots verts* (I eat green beans).

14 Vocabulary Man/*Monsieur Vocabulaire*

Step by step

1. Prepare a Vocabulary Man sheet in advance. Draw a man with a head, a torso, two arms and two legs. Number each part 1 to 6: 1 = head, 2 = torso, etc. Photocopy it (one sheet per group).

2. Decide on a list of six things for pupils to write. Concentrate on one topic or mix and match topics for revision. For example, for greetings, write on the board:

   1 = say hello to your teacher

   2 = say hi to a friend

   3 = ask 'how are you?'

   4 = say you're OK

   5 = say thank you

   6 = say goodbye to your teacher.

   (Answers: 1 = *Bonjour*, 2 = *Salut*, 3 = *Ça va ?*, 4 = *Ça va bien*, 5 = *Merci*, 6 = *Au revoir*.)

3. Give a sheet to each group. They write the words on the corresponding parts of the man.

4. For each section pupils complete correctly, they win the corresponding number of points. The first group to finish gets a bonus point. The group with most points wins.

Classroom management	Whole class/groups
Skill	Writing
Aim	To write familiar words from memory
Resources	Photocopies of blank Vocabulary Man activity sheets (one per group)

 Useful phrases

Complétez les sections de Monsieur Vocabulaire.

Complete the sections of the Vocabulary Man.

Comments

- This works well as revision of several topics or as homework. For example, ask pupils to come up with six possible challenges in class. Hand out a blank Vocabulary Man sheet to pupils and ask them to copy the challenges on each section. They complete the Vocabulary Man at home. Go through their work during the next lesson.

- You could also adapt the game to play with sounds.

 To increase the level of challenge, add more parts to the man: feet, hands, etc.

You could also increase the level of difficulty of each challenge: 1 = find one word, 2 = find two words, etc., or ask for phrases or full sentences.

Notes

15   Pass on the message/*Passe à l'autre*

Step by step

Classroom management	Whole class
Skill	Writing (and reading)
Aim	To write words from memory
Resources	Sheets of paper Adhesive tack

1. Decide on a topic for pupils to revise. For example, what pupils do in their spare time:

   je regarde la télé (I watch TV)

   je joue à un jeu vidéo (I play a video game)

   je fais du vélo (I ride a bike)

   je lis une BD (I read a comic)

   je fais de la peinture (I paint)

   je vais à la pêche (I go fishing)

   je tricote (I knit), etc.

2. Four pupils go out of the class.

3. A volunteer comes to the board and draws a pastime, e.g. a person knitting, on a sheet of paper which is tacked to the board.

4. Ask Pupil 1 to come in from outside. She looks at the drawing and writes underneath what she thinks it is. For example: *Je tricote* (I knit). She might get it wrong and think the person is painting, in which case, she will write: *Je fais de la peinture* (I paint).

   Leave the phrase, even if it is not the correct one, making sure it is mistake-free. (The class must remain silent.)

5. Remove the drawing but leave the phrase on the board. Then, tack a new blank sheet to the board.

6. Ask Pupil 2 to come in. He must read the phrase and draw a picture to match that on the sheet.

7. Rub out the phrase and leave the drawing. Repeat the same process with Pupils 3 and 4.

8. Compare the first and last drawings. If they are similar, the group scores four points. If they are not, and the message got lost along the line, the group scores two points, as long as their sentences were mistake-free.

9. To play another round, a different group (of four pupils) goes outside the room while a new volunteer chooses another phrase to draw. Repeat the process.

Dessine (un passe-temps).	Draw (a pastime) [to a single pupil].
Regarde le dessin.	Look at the drawing [to a single pupil].
Écris une phrase.	Write a sentence [to a single pupil].

Comments

- A variation of this game is to use mime instead of drawing. Four pupils go out of the room. One pupil from the class comes up to the board and writes a phrase, for example: *Je regarde la télévision.* Ask Pupil 1 to come in. He looks at the written phrase and thinks of a mime. Rub out the phrase. Ask Pupil 2 to come in. The whole class mimes the action to Pupil 2, who then writes the phrase on the board. Repeat the process with Pupils 3 and 4, and see what happens!

 To increase the challenge, ask pupils to read out and pronounce the phrases as correctly as they can.

Notes

....

....

....

....

....

....

....

....

....

....

....

16 Running dictation/*La dictée sportive*

Step by step

The aim of this game is for pupils to reconstruct a text by dictating chunks of it to each other. It works with any topic and at any level and revises vocabulary, grammar and spelling, as well as practising all four skills (listening, speaking, reading and writing).

Classroom management	Pair-work
Skill	Writing
Aim	To write sentences (also read, speak, listen and memorise)
Resources	Short text for dictation on several sheets of paper

1. Select a short text (it can be a dialogue, a short text from a course book, a song, a poem or made-up sentences) and make a few copies.

2. Stick the copies up around the walls of the classroom.

3. Divide the class into pairs. Pupil 1 is the 'runner': he runs to a text to read the first chunk (this might be a single word or a longer phrase). He must memorise it, run back to Pupil 2 (who is the 'writer'), and dictate what he remembers. The 'writer' writes it down.

4. They then swap roles. Pupil 2 runs to see the next chunk and runs back to dictate it to Pupil 1. They repeat the process until the text is completed.

5. When a pair finishes, they put up their hands. The winning pair is the team that finishes first, with a mistake-free text. If they have made mistakes, do not say what they are, just indicate how many mistakes there are. They must keep running to check until their text is perfectly correct.

> **Useful phrases**
>
> *Élève 1, cours chercher un morceau du texte.*
> Pupil 1, run to get a chunk of the text.
>
> *Élève 2, écoute bien et écris le texte.*
> Pupil 2, listen carefully and write down the text.
>
> *Changez de rôle.*
> Swap roles.

Comments

You can adapt the idea of running dictations in the following ways:

• Cut up a short text into sentences and display the sentences randomly around the classroom. Once pupils have all the sentences written down (see steps above), they both decide what the order of the sentences should be. This is good for practising word and sentence order.

- Set a time limit. The first pair to write a completed mistake-free text wins.
- You could divide the class into groups of three pupils: a 'runner', a 'writer' and a 'checker', whose role is to make sure the writer is not making mistakes.
- With younger or less able pupils, you could use single words, short phrases or idioms and stand-alone sentences. Alternatively, you could prepare a gapped worksheet on which the 'writer' just needs to fill in the missing words dictated by the 'runner'.

 To increase the level of challenge, increase the length or the difficulty of the text, or perhaps use a song or a short story that pupils are not familiar with. You could then play the song if you have audio equipment available, or read out the short story.

Notes

17 Guess what!/*Devine !*

Step by step

1. Divide the class into two teams. Each team writes a short sentence using the language of the topic to be practised or revised. For example, on the topic of food, they could write *Je mange une pomme* (I eat an apple). The other team must try to guess what that sentence is.

Classroom management	Whole class/teams
Skill	Writing
Aim	To write a sentence word by word
Resources	None

2. A pupil from each team writes the first word of their sentence on the board. For example: *Je*

3. The other team must discuss what the next word in the sentence could be and send a pupil to the board to write it. Team A starts. For example: *Je + mange*

4. If the word they chose is the correct one, it stays on the board and they have another go at guessing the third word, e.g. *Je + mange + un*

   If it's not the correct word, a pupil from Team B rubs it off and it is now Team B's turn to have a go at guessing Team A's sentence.

5. Repeat the process until the whole sentence is written correctly. The first team to work out their opponents' sentence and to write it correctly wins.

Useful phrases

Écrivez une phrase sur … (les repas).   Write a sentence about … (meal times).
Devinez la phrase de l'autre équipe.   Guess the other team's sentence.
Écrivez un mot à la fois.   Write one word at a time.

Comments

- For a bonus point, ask each team to read out the completed sentence correctly and to give its meaning in English.

To increase the level of challenge, the sentences could be a set number of words; for example:

between 5 and 7: *Il aime bien le chocolat* (he likes chocolate)

between 8 and 10: *Au petit déjeuner, ma petite sœur boit du lait* (at breakfast, my little sister drinks milk).

Alternatively, set an exact number of words.

18 Consequences/*Et alors...*

Step by step

1. Divide the class into groups of seven pupils if possible. Each group should have a sheet of paper and a pen.

2. Write the following writing frame on the board:

    1. *Il s'appelle ...*

    2. *Elle s'appelle ...*

    3. *Ils sont ... +* (place)

    4. *Ils +* (action verb)

    5. *Il dit ...*

    6. *Elle dit ...*

    7. *Alors ...*

Classroom management	Groups
Skill	Writing (and reading/listening)
Aim	To invent sentences using a writing frame
Resources	Paper and pens

3. Pupil 1 from each group copies the start of sentence 1 at the top of the sheet of paper and completes the sentence any way she likes. For example: *Il s'appelle Léo.*

4. Pupil 1 then folds the paper so the sentence is hidden and passes it on to Pupil 2, who fills in sentence 2 and so on, until the last pupil in the group has written her sentence.

5. When all the groups have finished writing, each one reads out their mini-story to the rest of the class.

6. The class decides which is the craziest story and that group gets a point!

> **Useful phrases**
>
> | | |
> |---|---|
> | *Regardez les débuts de phrase.* | Look at the sentence starters. |
> | *Complétez la première phrase.* | Complete the first sentence. |
> | *Pliez le papier et passez à votre voisin/voisine.* | Fold the paper and pass it to your neighbour. |
> | *Dépliez le papier et lisez l'histoire !* | Unfold the paper and read out the story! |

Comments

- A variation would be for groups to write the story collectively, without hiding what they write, in which case, the point is to make a story that makes sense as opposed to a nonsensical one. For example:

    1. *Il s'appelle Léo* (His name is Léo).

2. *Elle s'appelle Léa* (Her name is Léa).

3. *Ils sont au restaurant* (They are in a restaurant).

4. *Ils mangent un gâteau* (They are eating a cake).

5. *Il dit « J'aime bien le gâteau ».* (He says, 'I like the cake.')

6. *Elle dit « Moi, aussi ».* (She says, 'Me too.')

7. *Alors, ils commandent un autre gâteau !* (So they order another cake!)

 Increase the level of challenge by asking pupils to include a certain feature in all their sentences, such as an adjective or an adverb.

Notes

19 Paper ball battle/*La bataille en papier*

Step by step

1. Each pupil must write at least three things about themselves on a sheet of paper, but they must not write who they are. Depending on the topics you've covered, they could write about their physical appearance, family and pets, favourite pastimes, etc. For example:

Classroom management	Whole class
Skill	Writing (and reading)
Aim	To write sentences about yourself
Resources	Paper and pens

   J'ai dix ans. Je suis grand, mince et blond. J'ai des lunettes. (I'm ten. I'm tall, slim and blonde. I wear glasses.) Or *Je suis très sportive. Je joue au tennis et au hockey. J'adore aussi nager.* (I'm very sporty. I play tennis and hockey. I also love swimming.)

2. Go round the class to check that the sentences pupils have written are correct.

3. They then crumple their sheet of paper into a small ball and have a paper ball fight for a few seconds.

4. At your signal, they stop and each pupil picks up the paper ball nearest to them and unfolds it.

5. She reads out what is written on the paper and tries to work out who wrote it.

   P1: *C'est toi, Anya ?* (Is that you, Anya?)

   P2: *Oui, c'est moi* (Yes, that's me) or *Non, ce n'est pas moi !* (No, that's not me!).

6. If the pupil hasn't guessed, ask the rest of the class. If they can't work it out either, ask the writer to come forward and claim his paper. Repeat the process with other paper balls.

 Useful phrases

Écrivez trois choses sur vous.	Write three things about yourself.
Faites une boule avec la feuille.	Crumple the sheet into a ball.
Lancez la boule.	Throw the paper ball.
Ramassez la boule la plus proche.	Pick up the ball nearest to you.
Qui a écrit le message ?	Who wrote the message?

Comments

• The paper ball battle can be noisy, but need only last a few seconds!

 To increase the level of challenge, ask more advanced pupils to write a short paragraph using link words such as *et* and *mais*.

20 The lie detector/*Le détecteur de mensonge*

Step by step

1. Get each pupil in the class to write two or three things about themselves, one of which has to be a lie. Depending on the topics you've covered, it could be about family and pets, favourite hobbies, food they eat, and so on. For example:

   J'ai un frère et deux sœurs jumelles. Mon frère s'appelle Kevin, il a neuf ans. (I've got a brother and twin sisters. My brother is called Kevin and he's nine.)

Classroom management	Whole class/teams
Skill	Writing (and speaking/listening)
Aim	To write sentences about yourself
Resources	Optional: a buzzer (or bell, whistle, etc.)

2. Divide the class into two teams. Call one pupil from each team and give them a buzzer (it could be a bell, a whistle, anything that makes a noise. If you don't have anything to hand, they can just put up their hand).

3. Pupils volunteer to read out their sentences. The class must listen carefully until they've finished. The first pupil to buzz (or put up his hand) can say what he thinks the lie is. If he's right, the team wins a point. If not, the other team has a chance to guess and they score a point if they are right.

4. Repeat with other volunteers at the buzzer.

5. The team with most points at the end of the game wins.

Useful phrases

Écrivez deux ou trois choses sur vous.	Write two or three things about yourself.
Il faut écrire un mensonge.	You must include a lie.
Écoutez et trouvez le mensonge.	Listen and spot the lie.

Comments

- If pupils know each other very well, a variation is to write about other things. Ask pupils to do a bit of research at home, on the internet or at the library, and come up with two facts (one true and a false one they have made up) in French. For instance, they could write about Paris, French food, French-speaking countries, or people, things and places they know well, like your school, your town or a celebrity. They play the game as described above.

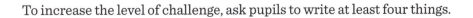

To increase the level of challenge, ask pupils to write at least four things.

Part 5: Numbers

Numbers are really useful, as they crop up in so many different situations. In French, the sound–spelling links for numbers 1–20 are particularly tricky so many of the games in this part will also be useful sounds practice.

You will find that there is more than one word in French for the English word 'number'. Basically:

- a one-digit number = *un chiffre*
- a number made up of two or more digits = *un nombre*
- a number (or specific numbers) in a sequence (e.g. telephone number, lottery number, etc.) = *un numéro*.

As well as the games here, you probably know lots of other number games. Why not try adapting games you use for numeracy, number bonds, etc. and playing them in French? This provides useful cross-curricular reinforcement of the concepts.

Many of the games from the other parts of this book can also be used to play with numbers. Games like Four corners/*Les quatre coins* (see page 4), Snap/*Bataille* (see page 82) or Find the pairs/*Trouvez les paires* (see page 84) can all be played with words and figures, for example.

1 Physical response games/*Jeux avec réponse physique*

Step by step

Once you have presented numbers, there are a variety of games in which pupils listen and show their comprehension in a physical way. The activities here are particularly good for beginners.

Classroom management	Whole class, small groups or pairs
Skill	Listening
Aim	To listen and respond
Resources	None

1. For numbers 1–10. You are the leader and stand at the front of the class. Call out a number and ask pupils to hold up the corresponding number of fingers. For a change, ask them to give the corresponding number of winks, stamps or finger clicks.

2. *Loto* (Bingo): Pupils write six different numbers from those they know, e.g. 2, 9, 11, 14, 16, 20. You are the leader and call the numbers. Pupils cross off a number when it is called. The first one with all numbers crossed off calls '*Loto*' and is the winner. Remember to keep a note of the numbers you call so you can check if a call is correct.

3. *Pair ou impair* (Odd or even): You are the leader and call a series of numbers. If a number is even, pupils sit/remain seated; if it is odd, they stand. If anyone does the wrong thing, they are out and come to the front of the class to help you spot anyone else who makes a mistake. The winner is the last pupil left in the game.

Useful phrases

Écoutez les chiffres.	Listen to the numbers.
Faites des clins d'œil/Tapez les pieds/ Cliquez les doigts.	Wink/Stamp your feet/ Click your fingers.
Si c'est un chiffre pair, asseyez-vous.	If it's an even number, sit down.
Si c'est un chiffre impair, levez-vous.	If it's an odd number, stand up.

Comments

- Be sure to present the numbers first. Introduce a few at a time: three is enough for very young children, while older groups could probably cope with five or six new numbers.

- These activities make good, quick starter activities.

 For speaking practice, pupils could play in pairs or small groups, taking turns to call the numbers.

2   Kitnakitna/*Kitnakitna*

Step by step

This game should be played in a hall or outdoors. The aim is to avoid being eliminated and be one of the final pairs to remain in the game.

1. Pupils stand in a space and, at your signal, jump on the spot.
2. Call a number, e.g.: '*Attention ... trois !*'
3. Pupils must form groups or chains comprising that number of children. They need to move quickly to avoid being left without a group.
4. Those players who are not in a group are out and sit at the side.
5. The game continues. Be sure to vary the numbers called, perhaps alternating odd and even numbers.

Classroom management	Whole class
Skill	Listening
Aim	To listen and respond to low numbers
Resources	None

Useful phrases

Sautez.	Jump up and down.
Écoutez le nombre.	Listen to the number.
Formez des groupes.	Get into groups.

Comments

- The unusual name for this game comes from an old Indian game on which it is based. Kitna means 'how much' or 'how many' in Hindi.
- The game is best for beginners as it is only practical with low numbers.

 To increase the challenge, you could also call '*Zéro*'. At this point, instead of finding a group, pupils have to roll up in a ball on the ground. The last one down is out. Pupils who are already out can be asked to check who is the slowest to react.

3   Read my mind/*Lisez dans mes pensées*

Step by step

1. You are the leader and stand at the front of the class. Tell pupils they are going to try to read your mind and predict the number you are thinking of. Write on the board

   plus +

   moins −

   to help them if you need to give 'clues'.

Classroom management	Whole class, small groups or pairs
Skill	Speaking and listening
Aim	To practise saying and understanding numbers
Resources	None

2. Place your hands on either side of your head in a dramatic fashion, as though thinking hard, and say:

   T: *Je pense à un chiffre. Qui peut deviner ce que c'est ?* (I'm thinking of a number. Who can guess what it is?)

3. Pupils put up their hand if they want to guess.

4. Choose a pupil to read your mind. She says a number. If the number is not right, provide a clue for the next guess by saying *plus* (more) or *moins* (less).

5. Continue until someone gets the right number.

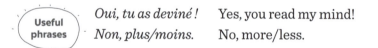

Useful phrases

Oui, tu as deviné !   Yes, you read my mind!

Non, plus/moins.   No, more/less.

Comments

- You could play in teams, with a point awarded for each correct guess.
- Once they understand the principle, pupils could play in small groups or pairs. Ask the child whose mind is being read to write their number on a small piece of paper and hide it in their pocket. This helps to avoid them changing their mind in the middle of the game!

Add a further challenge by asking the class to predict (in French) how many goes they will need to guess the number you are thinking of. They win if they guess it in fewer goes than predicted, or lose points if they go over.

4 Human noughts and crosses/
Le morpion vivant

Step by step

The aim of the game is to get three players from your team sitting in a line.

1. Arrange chairs in three rows of three
    to form the 'board'. (See below.)

2. Divide the class into two teams (one
    noughts, one crosses). Boys v. girls
    works well.

3. Show a player from the first team a
    flashcard with a number written on
    it in figures (or write it on the board). If that pupil
    can name the number correctly, he can go to sit on
    one of the chairs (he chooses which one).

4. Repeat the process with a pupil from the other
    team.

5. The first team to have a line of three team members
    sitting in a row scores a point.

6. Start the game again from scratch with different
    team members. Play until one team has scored five
    points.

Classroom management	Whole class
Skill	Speaking
Aim	To practise saying individual numbers
Resources	Nine chairs Optional: flashcards with numbers written as figures

 Useful phrases

Votre symbole, c'est le cercle/ la croix.	Your symbol is the nought/the cross [to a team].
C'est quel chiffre/nombre ?	Which number is it [to a single pupil]?
Choisis une chaise et assieds-toi.	Choose a chair and sit down [to a single pupil].

Comments

*   You can use the game to practise any sets of numbers, from 1–9 for beginners to larger, more complex numbers for older groups.

*   For a change, you could also play a more traditional noughts and crosses game, with a grid on the board, or with pupils playing in pairs with pen and paper. Start by drawing on the board a noughts and crosses grid containing figures.

<table>
<tr><td>10</td><td>12</td><td>20</td></tr>
<tr><td>14</td><td>16</td><td>18</td></tr>
<tr><td>11</td><td>13</td><td>15</td></tr>
</table>

- Choose an able pupil to come to the front and play against you. He can choose whether to take the nought or the cross symbol. You take turns to say a number in order to place your nought or cross, with the aim of making a line of three of your symbols. The winner is the first to make a row of three symbols, either vertically, horizontally or diagonally. Once you have modelled the game in this way, pupils could play in pairs.

 To make the game more challenging, set out rows of four × four chairs (or even five × five) so that pupils have to make a row of four or five team members.

You could also ask pupils to do simple sums, e.g.: 3 + 6, instead of showing them the numbers as figures.

Notes

....

....

....

....

....

....

....

....

....

....

....

....

....

....

5   Let me guess/*Devinez*

Step by step

1. Before pupils arrive, fill a container (or, if you have more than one, number them) with small objects such as pebbles, paper clips, rubber bands or pieces of dried pasta.

2. Let all the pupils have a good look at the container (no touching!).

3. Pupils write their estimate of how many items are in the container – they can write the word in French or just a figure.

4. Then, as a class, count the items out to see whose estimate was correct.

Classroom management	Whole class
Skill	Speaking (and writing)
Aim	To estimate how many items are in a container and count them to check
Resources	One or more small containers (screw-top jar, paper cup or similar) A number of small objects to fill the container(s), e.g. pebbles, rubber bands, paper clips

Useful phrases

Il y a combien (de cailloux/de trombones/d'élastiques) ?
Devinez.
Comptons ensemble.

How many (pebbles/paper clips/rubber bands) are there?
Guess.
Let's count together.

Comments

- The game works best when there are at least ten items in the container.

To increase the challenge, once pupils have counted the individual items, mix them up and put them back in the containers without pupils seeing what goes where. Then ask them to estimate again. For example:

Il y a huit cailloux, quinze trombones et vingt élastiques (There are eight pebbles, fifteen paper clips and twenty rubber bands).

6 Clapping game/*Claquez les doigts*

Step by step

1. All sit in a circle. Give each pupil a number, counting upwards from 1 (first pupil is *un*, second is *deux*, third is *trois,* etc.). Each person has nine lives.

Classroom management	Whole class
Skill	Listening and speaking
Aim	To practise recognising and saying numbers
Resources	None

2. Establish a rhythm of claps and finger clicks and get pupils to join in:

   clap, clap, click, click,

   clap, clap, click, click, etc.

3. Explain that, throughout the game, the rhythm will be kept going by all pupils in the class, at the same pace. You will start by calling a number as everyone clicks for the second time. The pupil with that number will be the next caller. After the next two claps, along with the first click, she repeats her own number, followed by a different number on the second click, and so on. For example:

   clap, clap, click, click + T: *Neuf.*

   clap, clap, click + P9: *Neuf,* click + P9: *Quinze.*

   clap, clap, click + P15: *Quinze,* click + P15: *Deux.*

4. If a pupil misses the rhythm or number, she loses a life.

5. The game starts again from the beginning. Start the rhythm again and call a new number.

6. If a player loses all nine lives, then the game is over. The winners are those with the fewest lives lost at the end of the game.

Useful phrases		
Battez les mains.	Clap your hands.
Claquez des doigts.	Click your fingers.
Répète ton chiffre/nombre.	Repeat your number.
Dis un autre chiffre/nombre.	Say a different number.

Comments

- If finger clicks are hard for younger children, they could tap their palms on their laps instead.

 To add more of a challenge, when a pupil slips up, ask all pupils to move one place to their right and take over the person's number (three will become four, four will become five, etc.). If numbers change often, it is hard to remember which number you are!

Notes

7 Unlucky thirteen/*Treize*

Step by step

Classroom management	Whole class
Skill	Speaking and listening
Aim	To practise counting
Resources	None

1. Pupils all stand, preferably in a circle. They must count round the class from 1 to 13. The aim of the game is to avoid being the person to say the unlucky number 13.

2. Each pupil can choose whether to say one, two or three numbers in the sequence. For example:

   P1: *un, deux*

   P2: *trois*

   P3: *quatre, cinq, six*

   P4: *sept, huit, neuf*, etc.

3. The pupil who has no option but to say '13' is out and must sit down. The counting starts again from 1.

4. The game continues until only one person is left standing.

Useful phrases

Mettez-vous debout.	Stand up.
On va compter.	We're going to count.
Dites un, deux ou trois chiffres/nombres.	Say one, two or three numbers.
Si vous dites « treize », vous avez perdu.	If you say '13', you've lost.
Assieds-toi.	Sit down [to a single pupil].

Comments

- Once you have introduced higher numbers, pupils could count every tenth number from 10 to 100, with 100 being the unlucky number: *dix, vingt, trente, quarante, cinquante, soixante, soixante-dix, quatre-vingts, quatre-vingt-dix, cent* (ten, twenty, thirty, forty, fifty, sixty, seventy, eighty, ninety, one hundred).

Increase the level of challenge by asking pupils to count backwards from 13 to 0.

In this game, the taboo number would be *zéro*.

8 Fizz, buzz/*Cocorico*

Step by step

1. Pupils stand and count round the class, each saying a number in turn. Every time there is a multiple of three (or five), they replace the number with the word *Cocorico* (Cock-a-doodle-doo).

   For example:

   P1: *un*

   P2: *deux*

   P3: *Cocorico*

   P4: *quatre*

   P5: *cinq*

   P6: *Cocorico*... etc.

Classroom management	Whole class or small groups
Skill	Speaking
Aim	To practise counting
Resources	None

2. If a pupil can't say the next number in the sequence, if he forgets to say *Cocorico* or says it in the wrong place, he is out and sits down.

3. The winner is the last pupil standing.

Useful phrases

On va compter.	We're going to count.
Chaque personne dit un nombre.	Each person says a number.
Si c'est un multiple de (trois), on ne dit pas le nombre, on dit « Cocorico ».	If it's a multiple of (three), you don't say the number, you say 'Cocorico'.

Comments

- This is a good cross-curricular activity for practising multiplication tables at the same time as French!

- To make this activity more competitive, divide the class into two teams. Each team counts in turn. The team with the most players still standing once a certain number, say thirty, is reached wins.

To increase the challenge, choose two numbers, each to be replaced with a different animal sound. For example, multiples of three could be *Cocorico* and multiples of five *oua oua* (pronounced *wa wa*), which is the sound a French dog makes (equivalent to *woof woof*).

9 Guess my age/*Devinez mon âge*

Step by step

1. Before the lesson, find a large picture of a famous person. Look up their date of birth on the internet and work out their age.

Classroom management	Whole class
Skill	Speaking (and listening)
Aim	To guess someone's age
Resources	Posters of famous people or large photos cut out of magazines

2. Show pupils the picture. If they know the vocabulary, you could ask questions such as:

   T: *Il/Elle s'appelle comment ?* (What's his/her name?)

   Il est acteur/chanteur/sportif, etc. ? (Is he an actor/singer/sports star, etc.?)

   Elle est actrice/chanteuse/sportive, etc. ? (Is she an actress/singer/sports star, etc.?)

   Il est français/anglais/américain, etc. ? (Is he French/English/American, etc.?)

   Elle est française/anglaise/américaine, etc. ? (Is she French/English/American, etc.?)

3. Finally ask each pupil in turn to guess the person's age. The youngest/least able can just say a number, but encourage those who can to put their estimate as a question to you, e.g.

   P: *Il/Elle a vingt-cinq ans ?* (Is he/she twenty-five?)

   Who gets it right?

Useful phrases

Regardez la photo.	Look at the photo.
À votre avis, il/elle a quel âge ?	In your opinion, how old is he/she?
En quelle année est-il né (or *est-elle née*) *?*	In what year was he (or she) born?

Comments

- Pupils might like to bring in their own pictures of famous people (and research their age/birthday) for a future lesson.

To increase the challenge, pupils could guess the star's birthday. For example:

P: *Son anniversaire est le vingt octobre ?* (Is his/her birthday on 20th October?)

The closest guess wins.

Alternatively, you could teach them the words *avant* (before) and *après* (after) so that you can provide clues to guide their guesses to the right answer.

10 Speed counting/*De plus en plus vite*

Step by step

1. To make sure pupils are comfortable counting in French, start by leading the class in counting aloud, as a chorus, different things in the classroom, e.g. doors, windows, chairs, desks, posters or pupils.

Classroom management	Whole class, groups or pairs
Skill	Speaking
Aim	To count quickly
Resources	Stopwatch

2. Pupils then work in pairs, practising counting a series of numbers as quickly as possible.

3. Time a few volunteers to see who can count the fastest. Times are only valid if the counter doesn't make any mistakes. Ask the class to listen carefully to make sure there are no slips.

Useful phrases

Comptez avec moi.	Count with me.
Il y a combien de portes/ fenêtres/chaises ?	How many doors/windows/ chairs are there?
Comptez le plus vite possible.	Count as quickly as possible.
Trois, deux, un … partez !	Three, two, one … go!

Comments

• To make this activity more exciting, offer an incentive for the class if everyone (or, with less able groups, maybe more than 80 per cent of the class) can beat the clock. The actual incentive will depend on your group and your circumstances (e.g. their choice of a song to sing at the end of the lesson, a sweet, house points).

Increase the challenge by asking pupils to count backwards, or by asking the counter to start counting (forwards or backwards) from a number you give him.

11 Ring the bell/*Le son de cloche*

Step by step

1. Place a small hand bell (or a tambourine, triangle or similar instrument that will make a sound) on the desk beside you.

2. Divide the class into two teams. They stand in parallel lines, facing the board.

3. The first pupil from each team steps forward. They should each be the same distance from the board and the same distance from the bell. Give each one a different coloured board marker.

Classroom management	Whole class
Skill	Listening and writing
Aim	To listen, understand and read numbers
Resources	Board and markers A hand bell (or tambourine or similar)

4. Call out a number or a simple sum. For example:

   T: *Quarante* (or *Quatre fois dix*).

5. Each pupil writes the number (or the number that is the answer to the sum) on the board, as a word rather than as a figure, and then rings the bell. The sound of the bell is the signal for the other pupil to stop writing.

6. A correct answer scores a team point. If the word is not correct, no points are scored.

7. Those two pupils move to the back of their lines and the next two in line take their place.

8. Try to let everyone have a turn. The winning team is the one with the most points at the end of the game.

 Useful phrases

Écoutez et écrivez.   Listen and write.

Puis, sonnez pour arrêter le jeu.   Then ring the bell to stop the game.

Comments

- To keep the whole class involved, tell pupils that they should all be working out in their head how to spell the number called (or doing the sum), as this is good practice for when they are at the front of the line. You might ask the same number more than once, and speed is important.

 You could insist on accurate spelling to win a point, or award one point for the right word and a bonus point if spelling is correct.

12 Auction/*Vente aux enchères*

Step by step

1. Before the lesson, cut out pictures of items to auction from a magazine and stick them onto cards. You could have pictures of cars, bikes, clothes, jewellery, toys, etc. Write what you think each item is worth on a sticky label and fix it to the back of the card. Then make a stack of paper euros (these could be simply €5, €10, €20, €50 written on small squares of paper).

2. Divide the class into groups of four or five pupils, and give each group the same amount of money.

Classroom management	Whole class, playing in groups
Skill	Speaking
Aim	To say different sums of money
Resources	Flashcards made with photos cut from magazines (5–10 items) Home-made paper euros or Monopoly money Sticky notes

3. The aim is to buy items at auction that have the highest total value (written on the back of the cards). Show each flashcard in turn and give pupils the chance to decide, in their groups, how much money they think it is worth/are willing to bid for it.

4. Start the auction by holding a flashcard in the air. Make sure pupils can't see the back of the card. Pupils call out their bids, starting low and building to the maximum they are prepared to bid. Only one person can bid per team. For example:

    T: *Une belle voiture de sport* ... (a beautiful sports car)

    P1: *Cent euros* (one hundred euros).

    P2: *Cent dix* (one hundred and ten).

    P3: *Cent trente* ... (one hundred and thirty), etc.

    The highest bid wins.

5. Continue in the same way with the other items. If a pupil has bid on behalf of his team already, he cannot bid again, in order to give everyone a chance.

6. Once all the items have been sold, pupils find the total value of their purchases by adding up the amounts on the notes on the back of their cards. They report back to the class – keep a note on the board – and the team with the highest-value items wins.

Useful phrases

Regardez ce beau/cette belle …	Look at this lovely …
Faites une offre !	Make a bid!
100 euros, une fois … deux fois …	100 euros, going once … going
adjugé, vendu !	twice … sold!

Comments

- This is good for practising high numbers. If pupils have only learned, say, up to 70, the items could all be real bargains: a car worth €69, etc.
- Make sure pupils understand that it may be more effective to win two or three small items rather than one big one, so they should not blow all their money on the first item.
- To make it more interesting, you could include some items with unlikely values, such as an ugly vase that is worth a fortune, etc.
- Keep the cards. You can reuse them with the same class at a later date: just change the values by adding different sticky notes.

For reading practice, you could make a little catalogue for each team, with a brief description of the item and the expected selling price range. For example:

Une guitare espagnole en bonne condition. Prix attendu: entre cinquante et soixante-dix euros. (A Spanish guitar in good condition. Expected price: between 50 and 70 euros.)

Notes

....

....

....

....

....

....

....

....

13 Tick-tock/*Tic-tac*

Step by step

1. Write on the board, in figures, the range of numbers you want pupils to practise, e.g. 1–31.

2. Pupils play in pairs. Pupil A says a number. Without hesitation, Pupil B says the number that follows. For example:

   PA: *Quinze* (15).

   PB: *Seize* (16).

3. Repeat several times to see if Pupil A can catch B out.

4. Swap roles so Pupil B says the number and A responds.

Classroom management	Pair-work
Skill	Listening and speaking
Aim	To practise saying numbers
Resources	None

Useful phrases

Élève A dit un nombre.	Pupil A says a number.
Élève B dit le nombre suivant.	Pupil B says the following number.
Sans hésiter !	Without hesitating!

Comments

- Alternatively, Pupil B could say the number that comes *before* the number that Pupil A calls. For example:

  PA: *Vingt* (20).

  PB: *Dix-neuf* (19).

- A similar but more demanding challenge for pupils who have learned numbers up to 99 is for Pupil A to call a two-figure number and Pupil B to reverse the figures. For example:

  PA: *Trente-six* (36).

  PB: *Soixante-trois* (63).

For older or more able pupils, have Pupil A say two numbers, e.g. *soixante-sept* (67) *et soixante et onze* (71). Pupil B must work out the difference, which here is *quatre* (4).

14 Maths for medals/*La course aux médailles*

Step by step

1. Divide the class into two teams. They stand in parallel lines, facing you. If there is an odd number of pupils in the class, one can come and stand by you and be the caller.

2. Throw the dice so that the two pupils at the front of the lines have a clear view. If you have a caller, she calls aloud – in French – the numbers thrown. If not, you can call.

Classroom management	Whole class
Skill	Speaking
Aim	To do simple sums
Resources	Two or three large foam dice Optional: home-made 'medals'

3. The two pupils at the front of the lines race to add together the numbers shown and call out the sum in French. For example:

   Caller: *Six ... plus cinq ... plus deux* (6 + 5 + 2).

   P1: *Treize !* (13).

4. The first to give the correct answer moves to the back of her line. The other pupil is out and goes back to his seat.

5. When only three pupils remain standing, they compete for the gold, silver and bronze medals. Throw the dice. The first to give the correct total wins gold.

6. Throw again. The faster of the final two wins silver, and the bronze medal is awarded to the third.

Useful phrases

Regardez les dés.	Look at the dice.
Additionnez les points le plus vite possible.	Add up the dots as quickly as possible.
Bravo, retourne en fin de la file.	Well done; go to the back of the line [to a single pupil].
Trop lent(e), tu es éliminé(e).	Too slow, you're out [to a single pupil].

Comments

- To keep the whole class involved, remember to tell pupils that they should all be adding the numbers called in their head as quickly as possible, as this is good practice for when they are at the front of the line.

- It gives the game more purpose if you can provide medals for the winners. You could make medals by cutting circles of cardboard and colouring them, or covering with tinfoil, and fixing them to a length of ribbon.

 Increase the challenge by having three or four lines so that pupils have more turns at competing.

Notes

15 Only numbers/*Entourez les nombres*

Step by step

1. Before pupils arrive, write on the board, dotted about in jumbled order, a mix of words, some numbers, some not. For example:

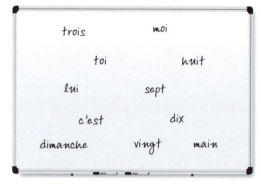

Classroom management	Whole class, in teams
Skill	Reading
Aim	To read numbers
Resources	Board marker

2. Play class v. teacher. Volunteers take turns to come and circle a word, but they can only circle if the word is a number. If they are correct, they score a point for the class. If they are wrong, it's a point for you.

Useful phrases

Entoure un nombre. — Circle a number [to a single pupil].

Uniquement les nombres. — Only numbers.

Comments

- Once all the numbers have been circled, you could use the words to play a different game. Ask everyone to close their eyes and then rub out two or three of the numbers. Pupils open their eyes and try to recall what the missing numbers are.

For writing practice, pupils could make similar puzzles to swap with their partners. They write twenty words dotted around on a sheet of paper, half are numbers and half are not. Can their partner circle all the number words?

16 On the clothesline/*La corde à linge*

Step by step

1. Divide the class into groups of four or five pupils.

2. Give each group some A4 sheets of paper (at least one per pupil), pens and scissors, a length of string to be *la corde à linge* (the clothesline) and some clothes pegs.

3. Draw a simple outline of a T-shirt on the board and ask pupils to copy it, large, on their sheets of paper, and then cut it out. They will need one T-shirt for each number in the set you are teaching (ten numbers is a decent maximum). For example:

4. Write the numbers you want to practise on the board in words. These should be words pupils have already met, not completely new numbers. For example:

   onze (11), *douze* (12), *treize* (13), *quatorze* (14), *quinze* (15), *seize* (16)

   Pupils study them for a minute or two to memorise the spelling.

5. Rub out the words and replace them with figures. Ask pupils to write a different number (spelling it out in full, not just the figure) on each T-shirt in pencil. For example:

6. When all the T-shirts are ready, check them for spelling. If any are wrong, ask the class to help to correct. Pupils go over the words in pen.

7. Each group shuffles their sheets and places them face down on the desk.

8. Two pupils from the group hold the ends of their string and pull the washing line taut.

Classroom management	Groups
Skill	Writing and reading
Aim	To write and read numbers and arrange them in numerical order
Resources	A4 paper Pencils and pens Scissors String Clothes pegs

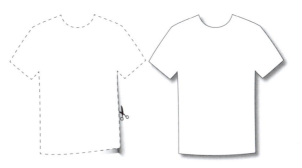

9. At a signal from you, all the groups take up their T-shirts and peg them on the clothesline in numerical order.

They compete to see which team can finish first. The pupils holding the string should also be actively involved in suggesting which numbers go where.

Useful phrases

Dessinez un T-shirt.	Draw a T-shirt.
Écrivez un chiffre/nombre.	Write a number.
Mettez les T-shirts sur la corde dans le bon ordre.	Hang the clothes on the line in the right order.
Dépêchez-vous !	Hurry up!

Comments

- More able or older pupils could draw the outlines of different items of clothing, and you could revise clothes vocabulary at the same time.

For more of a challenge, use higher numbers or make price tags, such as *douze euros soixante-dix* (twelve euros seventy).

Notes

....

....

....

....

....

17 Spider/*L'araignée*

Step by step

This game is based on the traditional game of Pizza. It is a pencil and paper spelling game for two players, but you could also play class v. teacher first, to provide pupils with a model.

Classroom management	Whole class or pairs
Skill	Reading and writing
Aim	To read and write numbers
Resources	Paper and pens or pencils

1. Pupil A thinks of a number and writes a row of dashes, each one representing one letter of the word. For example, if A is thinking of the number 25 (*vingt-cinq*), she writes

    _ _ _ _ _ ¯ _ _ _ _

2. Pupil B (the guesser) suggests a letter he thinks might be in the word. Pupil A writes that letter in, each time it occurs. For example, if the guesser suggests the letter 'i':

    _ *i* _ _ _ ¯ _ *i* _ _

3. If the suggested letter is not in the word, Pupil A draws one element of a spider (there are ten elements: head + body + eight legs).

4. The guesser wins the game if he can complete the word and write the number alongside as a figure before the spider is complete. Pupil A wins if she completes the spider before the guesser has spelled out the number.

Useful phrases

Élève A pense à un chiffre/nombre et fait des traits.

Un trait pour chaque lettre.

Élève B essaie d'épeler le chiffre/nombre.

Pupil A thinks of a number and draws dashes.

One dash for each letter.

Pupil B tries to spell the number.

Comments

- Obviously, pupils need to be familiar with the alphabet in French, and you may need to revise this first.
- Before you start, you could discuss which letters pupils think will occur most frequently (for example, vowels), so that they don't waste their guesses.
- To support spelling, write a list of numbers on the board (figure + French word) before pupils arrive:

  11 *onze,* 12 *douze,* etc.
- If you want to allow pupils more guesses, they could add two more features to the spider, e.g. eyes.

 Increase the level of challenge by allowing the guesser to suggest only consonants, or by allowing only a single vowel to be suggested.

Notes

18 Simple sums/*Champion de calcul*

Step by step

Classroom management	Pairs or individuals
Skill	Reading and writing
Aim	To read and complete simple sums
Resources	Paper and pen

1. If you feel pupils will need help with spelling, write a list of numbers on the board (figure + French word) before they arrive:

   11 *onze*

   12 *douze*

   13 *treize*

   14 *quatorze*, etc.

2. Individually or in pairs, pupils write twenty simple sums, using French words rather than figures. For example:

   huit + neuf =   *trente + un – onze =*

3. Pupils swap their sums with a partner and, at a signal from you, they all race to complete the sums.

4. As each pupil finishes, he puts up his hand and you award him a number – if there are twenty pupils in the class, the first finished is number 20, the next is 19 and so on, down to number 1 for the last pupil. (Alternatively, you could halt calculations once the first three pupils are finished.)

5. Check answers and give each pupil a mark out of twenty. If there is a tie for first place, high scorers add their finishing-place number to their score, and the highest score overall wins.

Useful phrases

Écrivez vingt opérations.	Write twenty sums.
Huit plus neuf égalent dix-sept.	Eight plus nine equals seventeen.
Échangez vos opérations.	Swap your sums.

Comments

- Write a few sums on the board first so that pupils see exactly what they are expected to do.
- For younger pupils, ten sums will be enough.

Ask more able or older pupils to include simple multiplication and division sums, e.g.

deux (fois) onze = … (2 × 11 = …)

douze (divisé par) deux = … (12 ÷ 2 = …)

19 Anagrams/*Les anagrammes*

Step by step

1. Once pupils are confident under-standing, speaking and reading a set of numbers, you could use anagrams to encourage them to write the num-bers correctly. Write a series of jum-bled letters on the board, enclosed in a circle or square. Choose letters that when unscrambled spell out a number. For example:

2. Pupils copy the letters from each circle onto a piece of paper. Then they unscramble them and write down the word they spell out. They can do this individually or in pairs.

3. Pupils could do this against the clock, if you want to make the activity competitive.

4. Check answers with the class.

Classroom management	Individuals
Skill	Writing
Aim	To write numbers
Resources	Paper and pens

Useful phrases	*Les lettres sont brouillées.*	The letters are jumbled up.
	Mettez les lettres en ordre pour écrire un chiffre/nombre.	Arrange the letters in the right order to make a number.

Comments

• Pupils could also compile their own anagrams to swap with a partner.

 To increase the challenge, ask pupils to add up the numbers in the circles. The first one to give you the correct total in French is the winner.

20 Number shoot-out/*Le duel des nombres*

Step by step

1. Choose two pupils to take part in the shoot-out. They stand and face each other.

2. If you want to revise numbers up to 31, for instance, call out a number in French. The two pupils compete to call out the number needed to add up to 31. For example:

   T: *Trois* (3).

   P1: *Vingt-huit* (28).

3. When a call is made, ask the class if they agree it is correct.

4. The pupil who gives the correct number scores a point and remains standing. The loser sits down and is replaced by another challenger.

5. The winner is the pupil with the most points at the end of the game.

Classroom management	Whole class
Skill	Listening and speaking
Aim	To do a simple calculation in French (e.g. number bonds)
Resources	None

Useful phrases

Qu'est-ce qu'il faut ajouter pour faire 31 ?	Which numbers do you need to add to make 31?
Tu gagnes, tu rejoues.	You win – you can play again [to a single pupil].
Tu perds, tu t'assieds.	You lose – you sit down [to a single pupil].

Comments

- You can adjust the target number, depending on which set of figures you want to practise.

- You could let a volunteer call out the number in your place.

- Number recipes are a useful warm-up for this, or if you'd like to introduce some writing practice. Pupils work in pairs to list a variety of ways (recipes) to make up a total which you set. For example, if the number you set is 24 *(vingt-quatre)*, they might write:

  vingt plus quatre (20 + 4)   *trois fois huit* (3 × 8)

  trente moins six (30 – 6)   *quarante-huit divisé par deux* (48 ÷ 2)

To make the game more challenging, ask pupils to add two further numbers to add up to 31.

For example:

T: *Dix* (10).

P: *Quinze et six* (15 + 6).

Part 6: Grammar

Grammar is at the heart of a language. Understanding grammatical patterns and knowing how a language works puts you in control, so it is worth spending time getting to grips with it. With children, games can help reinforce grammatical patterns in a positive and engaging way. They allow pupils to focus on the details of the rules of grammar almost without realising it.

As well as the games here, a number of the games from other parts of the book can be adapted to practise specific points of grammar, in particular:

Part 1: Listening – games 3, 7, 9, 14

Part 2: Speaking – games 4, 8, 13, 14

Part 3: Reading – games 1, 6, 7, 8, 10, 13, 14, 19

Part 4: Writing – games 3, 4, 10, 11, 12.

1 Zoé's ark/*L'arche de Zoé*

Step by step

This game is loosely based on the story of Noah's ark. The 'world of words' is threatened and Zoé calls for different types of words to come onto her ark to be saved. Pupils must board two by two; they can't go on board without a partner. The game helps reinforce the pupils' literacy work.

Classroom management	Whole class
Skill	Grammar (reading)
Aim	To recognise word types
Resources	Word cards Optional: audio equipment to play music

1. In advance, prepare cards with French words belonging to different word types (with an even number of words, so that pupils can pair up), depending on what you have already covered with your pupils. For example:

   determiners: *un, une, des, le, la, les* (a, the)

   nouns: *ballon, table, pommes, copains* (balloon, table, apples, friends)

   proper nouns: *Papa, Maman, Paul, Madame Bernard* (Mum, Dad, other names of people)

   adjectives: *grand/grande, petit/petite, rouge* (big, small, red)

   verbs: *jouer, écouter, parler, écrire* (to play, to listen, to speak, to write)

   adverbs: *lentement, rapidement, doucement,* (slowly, quickly, softly)

   pronouns: *je, tu, il, elle, nous, vous, ils, elles* (I, you (singular), he, she, we, you (plural), they).

2. Give one card to each pupil (even number). They must read the word on their card, walk around the room and pair up with someone who has a word in the same category as them.

3. If you can, play some music while pupils are doing this. Stop the music (or give a signal) and name a category to come on board.

4. Pupils come to you two by two. Check their cards: if a pair is correct, they get on board; if not, they go back. Repeat the process with the other word categories.

> **Useful phrases**

Lisez votre carte.	Read your cards.
Trouvez quelqu'un pour faire une paire.	Find someone to make a pair.
Il faut deux mots de la même catégorie.	You need two words of the same type.

Comments

- If you have an odd number of pupils in the class, ask one to be Zoé. If not, you can be Zoé.
- Play this game in a hall if you can, as children will need space to move around and it's going to be noisy.

- You could adapt this game to practise other grammar points: feminine/masculine words, singular/plural words, nouns/matching determiners, nouns/matching adjectives, personal pronouns/verb forms, etc.

 You can vary the level of challenge: for younger pupils, have word cards listing only determiners and nouns, and they must pair up according to gender, for example: *un ballon/un vélo* (a balloon/a bike); *une raquette/une voiture* (a racket/a car), etc.

To increase the challenge, use completely new words: pupils need to work out what type of words they are (using strategies such as looking at word endings).

Notes

2   Tongue-tied/*La langue paralysée*

Step by step

1. Pupils divide into pairs. Explain that they are doctors whose job it is to cure you of a serious problem: you become tongue-tied when you try to say certain words. Their mission is to be the first pair to cure you by working out what types of words you can't say.

Classroom management	Whole class/pairs
Skill	Grammar (listening/reading)
Aim	To recognise word types
Resources	A text (from a textbook, story book, poem, song, etc.)

2. Write a short text on the board, for example, a short rhyme (see list of rhymes on page 245):

   Je mets mon manteau,

   Je mets mon chapeau,

   Je fais du judo,

   C'est rigolo.

3. Read it aloud but do not read out the verbs. Close your mouth and say 'mmmmm' instead when you come to a verb. For example:

   Je « mmmmm » mon manteau, Je « mmmmm » mon chapeau, Je « mmmmm » du judo,

   C' « mmmmm » rigolo.

4. In pairs, pupils confer and write down their diagnosis. Then they join up with another pair and confer in groups of four. If they don't agree, they have to discuss and come up with one final diagnosis.

5. Ask each group of four to tell the class their diagnosis. For example, here: you're tongue-tied on verbs. Give one point to each pair who made a correct diagnosis.

6. Repeat the process with a different type of words. For example:

   Je mets mon « mmmmm », Je mets mon « mmmmm », Je fais du « mmmmm », C'est rigolo.
   (nouns)

   The pair with most points wins.

> **Useful phrases**
>
> | | |
> |---|---|
> | *Écoutez et suivez le texte.* | Listen and follow the text. |
> | *Je ne dis pas quelle catégorie de mots ?* | What word type don't I say? |

Comments

- The aim of this type of game is to generate discussion about language and grammar.
- You can adapt this to all sorts of words and language points depending on the level of the class. For instance, you could read all the nouns in a text except the feminine ones or those in the plural.
- You could ask volunteers to read aloud a text and become tongue-tied on certain types of word.

 To increase the level of challenge, choose a text that pupils are very familiar with, but don't show it to them. They must listen and work out the type of words you are not saying.

Notes

3 Smurfing/*Schtroumpfant*

Step by step

The aim of the game is to call on pupils' prior knowledge of word types to get them to guess what a mystery word is, as well as to generate discussion about language and grammar.

Classroom management	Whole class/pairs
Skill	Grammar (listening/reading)
Aim	To recognise word types
Resources	None

1. Choose simple sentences (revising known language) replacing one of the words with the word *'schtroumpf'*. Read them out or write them on the board. For example:

   *Je « schtroumpf » au football. (joue/*I play football)

   *Elle « schtroumpf » les légumes, c'est super ! (aime/adore/*She loves vegetables, they're great!)

   *Moi, j'aime les « schtroumpf », surtout les pommes. (fruits/*I like fruit, especially apples)

   *Un chihuahua, c'est un « schtroumpf » chien. (petit/*A chihuahua is a small dog).

2. Pupils divide into pairs. When each pair has worked out the mystery word, they join up with another pair and confer. If they agree on the word, they put their hands up. If they don't agree, they have to discuss and come up with one final decision.

3. Ask each group of four to tell you what their guess is. Give one point to each pair with a correct word.

4. Repeat the process. The pair with most points wins.

Useful phrases

Devinez le mot français pour « schtroumpf ». Guess the French word for 'schtroumpf'.

Comments

- This game, often played in France, is based on *Les Schtroumpfs* (the Smurfs), a series of comic characters created by the Belgian cartoon artist Peyo who use the word *schtroumpf* when they speak.

- Pupils might work out the correct word type but not the exact word. In that case, they can have several guesses. For example: *Mon chat est « schtroumpf ». (*My cat is ...), they can suggest adjectives: *petit, gros, noir* (small, fat, black).

You could ask pupils to write a sentence replacing one word with *schtroumpf*. Ask volunteers to read out their sentence to the class, who work out the mystery word.

4 Beetle drive/*Le cochon qui rit*

Step by step

Le cochon qui rit (the laughing pig) is the French name for the traditional beetle game. The aim of the game is to be the first player to draw a complete beetle (or pig, as the case may be!). The parts you are allowed to draw are determined by the throw of the die. Players must get *all* the parts in order: that is, they must get 1 on the die to get part number 1, 2 to get part number 2, etc. in that order.

Classroom management	Pair-work
Skill	Grammar (writing)
Aim	To practise common adjectives (agreement and position)
Resources	Per pair of pupils: one die, one photocopy of the pig drawing

1. In advance, do a simple drawing of a pig, with different parts numbered 1 to 6, and make photocopies (one per pair). Add a key. For example:

   1 – *C'est*

   2 – *un/une*

   3 – adjective

   4 – noun

   5 – adjective

   6 – full stop.

2. Write a list of vocabulary on the board to support younger learners. They select words for sections 3, 4 and 5 from that list. For example:

   Throw a 3: adjectives = *beau/belle, gros/grosse, petit/petite* (beautiful, large, small)

   Throw a 4: nouns = *grenouille* (f), *sorcière* (f), *monstre* (m), *roi* (m) (frog, witch, monster, king)

   Throw a 5: adjectives = *vert/verte, méchant/méchante, rigolo/rigolote* (green, nasty, funny).

3. Divide the class into pairs and hand out a die and a photocopy of the pig to each pair.

4. Each pair plays the game, choosing words on the board for sections 3, 4 and 5. They must be careful to choose a noun that matches the determiner they've chosen, and adjectives that match the gender of the noun. They write the words and the punctuation in each section of the pig as they win it.

5. When a pair has completed the pig and written a sentence, they put up their hands and read out their sentence. For example: *C'est un gros monstre vert.* If their sentence is correct,

they win. If not, explain which word was wrong. They carry on the game, rolling the die to change that word. The first pair to complete the pig and make a correct sentence wins.

Lancez le dé.	Throw the die.
Avec un 3/5, choisissez un adjectif.	With a 3/5, choose an adjective.
Avec un 4, choisissez un nom.	With a 4, choose a noun.

Comments

- Encourage the whole class to pay attention when a pair is reading out their sentence, as it could help them to make nouns and adjectives agree correctly when it is their turn.

To increase the level of challenge, provide vocabulary support but mix all the words up so that pupils need to select the correct word type and know which adjectives go in front of the noun and which go after it.

For more challenge and more creativity, do not provide any vocabulary support: pupils must come up with their own nouns and adjectives.

Notes

....

....

....

....

....

....

....

....

....

....

....

5   All aboard!/*Tous en bus !*

Step by step

The aim of the game is to revise prepositions of place; for example, *devant, derrière, à côté de, en face de, à gauche de, à droite de* (in front, behind, next to, opposite, to the left of, to the right of).

Classroom management	Whole class/teams
Skill	Grammar (listening)
Aim	To practise prepositions of place
Resources	Chairs

1. Set out chairs in rows to represent seats in a bus, with one seat in front for the driver (on the left-hand side, as it's a French bus!). There should be the same number of chairs as there are players in the team.

2. Divide the class into two teams of 'passengers'. Team A starts: they line up as if queuing for the bus and carefully listen to your instructions; for example:

    T: *Emily, assieds-toi <u>devant</u>, tu es le chauffeur.* (Emily, sit in front, you're the driver.) *Kevin, mets-toi <u>derrière</u> Emily.* (Kevin, go behind Emily), etc.

    They choose their seat accordingly. Their teammates must not help them.

3. Tell Team B to watch very carefully, because if they spot a pupil from Team A not sitting in the right place, they can stop the game and challenge them. If they make a correct challenge, that pupil must get off the bus.

4. Once the last pupil in Team A has had their turn, make a note of the number of passengers correctly seated in the bus.

5. Repeat the process with Team B. The team with the most passengers in the right place wins!

Useful phrases

Écoutez bien les instructions.   Listen carefully to instructions.
Puis trouvez votre siège.   Then find your seat.

Comments

- You could play the game in two parts, part 1 as above and part 2 as follows: pupils take their schoolbags on board the bus. Once you've told them where to sit, ask them to follow your instructions as to where to put their bags. For example:

Pose ton sac sous ton siège/à côté de toi/sur tes genoux (Place your bag under your seat/next to you/on your lap).

 To increase the linguistic challenge, ask 'passengers' to say a sentence to describe where they are sitting, using a preposition. For example: *Je suis à côté de Lucie* (I'm next to Lucie).

Notes

....

....

....

....

....

....

....

....

....

....

....

....

....

....

6   Living sentence/*La phrase vivante*

Step by step

Play this game to introduce and practise the position of certain words in a French sentence; for example, adjectives or negatives.

Classroom management	Groups
Skill	Grammar (reading and speaking)
Aim	To practise word order
Resources	Word flashcards

1. Prepare some sentences (there should be one per group once you've divided the class into groups of about six pupils). Write the individual words of each sentence on flashcards in advance (they need to be large enough to read at the front of the class). For example:

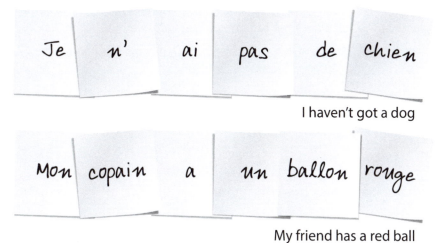

I haven't got a dog

My friend has a red ball

2. Divide the class into groups and give each group a set of cards. They must each take a card and then stand up and arrange themselves to make up the sentence in the correct order.

3. When a group has finished, they sit down. Make a note of who finishes first.

4. When all the groups are finished, ask the group who finished first to come to the front, stand in a line in order and read out their sentence. If they are correct, they win X points for finishing first and correctly (X = the number of groups). Then ask the next group, who get X – 1 points, and so on. If they have made a mistake, they don't get any points (or award half marks if they can correct it).

Useful phrases

Chaque élève tient une carte.	Each pupil holds a card.
Mettez-vous dans le bon ordre	Arrange yourselves in the right
pour faire une phrase correcte.	order to make up a sentence.
Chacun lit son mot.	Everyone reads their word.

Comments

- If there are fewer pupils than cards in a group, some pupils can hold two cards. If there are more pupils than cards, make sure pupils without a card in one round take part in the next one.

- It is in pupils' interest to watch carefully when groups come to the front to read out their sentences, as they will be getting those sentences to rearrange at some stage in the game!

To increase the level of challenge, set a time limit. Hand out the cards face down. Give a signal for groups to turn over their cards and start the timer. Groups who complete their sentences correctly before the time is up get an extra point.

To increase the linguistic challenge, make longer sentences and use exceptions, such as French adjectives that are placed before nouns. For example:

[Mon] [petit] [frère] [n'] [a] [pas] [de] [baskets] [blanches] (My little brother hasn't got any white trainers).

Notes

....

....

....

....

....

....

....

....

....

7   Human tetris/*Le tétris humain*

Step by step

1. Divide the class into two teams. Team A is on one side of the room, Team B on the other. Explain that the aim of the game is for Team A to make a correct sentence (made up of three or more words) from 'travelling words' which pupils from Team B will be saying aloud while walking towards Team A.

Classroom management	Whole class/teams
Skill	Grammar (speaking and listening)
Aim	To practise word order
Resources	None

Pupils in Team A need to listen carefully and decide where a word fits in a sentence. They nominate one pupil to direct that 'travelling word'. There must be as many pupils from Team A directing as there are 'travelling words' walking towards them.

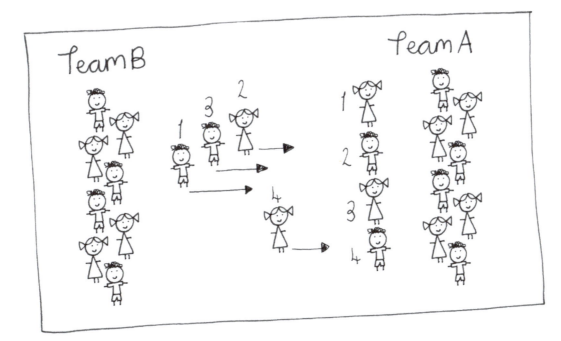

2. Go to Team B and whisper this sentence: *Il mange une pomme* (He is eating an apple).

   Pupil 1 from Team B starts walking, saying aloud « *mange* », then Pupil 2 starts walking saying « *il* », then Pupil 3, who says « *pomme* », and finally Pupil 4, with « *une* ».

One pupil from Team A must attract the attention of the pupil saying the word *mange*.

For example:

P1: *Mange, viens ici. Mange, ici, ici !* (*Mange*, come here. *Mange*, here, here!)

A second pupil from Team A attracts the attention of the pupil saying *il* and places herself on the left of the pupil calling for *mange*.

P2: *Il, viens ici. Ici, il, ici !*

And so on, until there is one pupil from Team A for each 'word' from Team B.

3. When all the travelling words have arrived and 'docked' as directed, get pupils from Team A to read out the sentence. They win as many points as there are words correctly placed.

4. It's now Team A's turn to be given a sentence and for Team B to order words correctly. Another set of pupils play. The team with most points at the end of the game wins.

Useful phrases

Marche vers l'autre équipe.	Walk towards the other team.
Dis ton mot tout fort.	Say your word aloud.
Suis les instructions de l'autre équipe.	Follow the other team's instructions.
Appelle un mot vers toi.	Call one word towards you.
Place-toi au bon endroit dans la phrase.	Position yourself correctly in the sentence.

Comments

- This game is best played in a hall as it needs space. It is loosely based on the principle of the classic video game, Tetris: here, there are no blocks falling down from the top to reorder at the bottom, but 'travelling words' that players from the opposite team must control so that they reach their correct place in a sentence.

Increase the level of challenge by increasing the length of sentences. Use words like adjectives and negative phrases that go in different places in French and English sentences.

Tell the 'travelling words' to walk faster as the game progresses!

Notes

....

....

....

8 Triplets/*Les triplés*

Step by step

1. Prepare three sets of cards in advance, using language pupils are familiar with:

   one set of determiners (masculine and feminine)

   one set of nouns (with their gender)

   one set of adjectives (neutral).

   For example:

   Determiners: *un, une/le, la* (a/the)

   Nouns (e.g. zoo animals): *singe* (m), *tortue* (f), *girafe* (f), *hippopotame* (m) (monkey, turtle, giraffe, hippopotamus). Show the gender by the letter 'm' or 'f' (or colour code words, e.g. red for feminine, blue for masculine, if you normally use colour coding).

   Adjectives: *marron, féroce, jaune, timide* (brown, fierce, yellow, shy).

Classroom management	Whole class
Skill	Grammar (reading)
Aim	To practise word order (determiner + noun + adjective), gender (and number)
Resources	Word cards Optional: audio equipment to play music

2. Give each pupil a card. Play some French music: pupils walk or skip around the class (or hall) until you stop the music (or until they hear your signal).

3. They must then make groups of three, comprising a determiner, a noun and an adjective. The first group to get together comes and lines up at the front of the class, the second group goes behind the first, and so on.

4. Ask the first group to read out their three cards. For example: *le + singe + féroce*. If they get them in the correct order, they get one point, plus three bonus points for being the first group. The second group will get two bonus points and the third group one bonus point. Ask groups who don't make the correct phrases to think again and then rearrange themselves.

5. Collect in the cards, shuffle them and hand them out again to different pupils. Repeat steps 2–4 for another round of the game. Each pupil keeps track of his score. Is there an overall winner?

Useful phrases

| *Formez des groupes de trois.* | Make up groups of three. |
| *Il faut un déterminant, un nom et un adjectif.* | You must have a determiner, a noun and an adjective. |

Comments

- This game is better played in a hall or outdoors as pupils need space to move around and it may be noisy.

 To increase the level of linguistic challenge, add cards which will make pupils work on gender and number. For example:

Determiners: *le, la, les, un, une, des, l'*

Nouns (e.g. zoo animals): *tigre* (m), *tortue* (f), *éléphant* (m), *girafe* (f), *lion* (m), *hyènes* (plural), *singes* (plural) (tiger, tortoise, elephant, giraffe, lion, hyenas, monkeys)

Adjectives: *féroce* (fierce), *verte* (green), *gris* (grey), *jaune* (yellow), *paresseux* (lazy), *méchantes* (nasty), *rigolos* (funny).

Only accept triplet phrases that are grammatically correct, with adjectives matching the nouns in gender and number.

Notes

....

....

....

....

....

....

....

....

....

....

....

9   Dice race/*La course aux dés*

Step by step

1. Divide the class into groups of three or four. Each group should have a sheet of paper per pupil, one six-sided die and one pen.

2. Write six infinitives on the board (or more, depending on the level of the class). For example, for regular verbs ending in *-er*: *aimer, parler, jouer,*

Classroom management	Groups
Skill	Grammar (writing)
Aim	To practise conjugating verbs
Resources	Dice Paper and pens

chanter, danser, écouter (to love, to speak, to play, to sing, to dance, to listen). As you write each one, ask pupils to tell you the English equivalent. If you think pupils need support, you could also write out one present-tense verb conjugation, as a model for pupils, e.g.

Regarder = to look at

je regarde (I look)

tu regardes (you (singular) look)

il/elle/on regarde (he/she/they looks/look)

nous regardons (we look)

vous regardez (you (plural) look)

ils/elles regardent (they look)

3. On your signal, one pupil in each group starts rolling the die until she gets a 6. Then she immediately picks up the pen and starts writing the conjugation of one (or more) of the verbs listed on the board on her sheet of paper, until Pupil 2 takes the pen from her.

4. The moment Pupil 1 drops the die to start writing, Pupil 2 picks it up and rolls it (while Pupil 1 is writing) until he gets a 6. At that point, Pupil 2 grabs the pen from Pupil 1 and starts his own conjugation. The moment Pupil 2 drops the die, Pupil 3 picks it up and rolls it to try to get a 6, and so on.

The winner in each group is the pupil with most verbs correctly conjugated. Who is the overall winner in the class?

Useful phrases

Lancez le dé pour faire un six.   Throw the die to get a 6.

Conjuguez les verbes sur votre feuille.   Start conjugating the verbs on your sheet.

Comments

- A variation on conjugating with dice: Write the numbers 1 to 6 in two columns, A and B, on the board. In column A, write six different verbs in the infinitive. In column B, write six different subject pronouns.

	A	B
1		
2		
3		
4		
5		
6		

Pupils play in teams. One pupil from Team A rolls a die to determine the verb and the second die to determine the subject. If he conjugates the verb correctly (orally or in writing), the team wins the total of the points shown on the dice. If he makes a mistake, the team doesn't score any points. Repeat with a pupil from Team B until all pupils from both teams have had a go. Add up the points for each team, and the one with most points wins.

 With younger pupils, limit this to the pronouns you have already covered (for example, *je* and *tu*) and provide a few more verbs.

Notes

....

....

....

....

....

....

10 Hop to it!/*Et que ça saute !*

Step by step

Classroom management	Whole class/teams
Skill	Grammar (writing)
Aim	To practise conjugating verbs
Resources	Timer/stopwatch Board pens

1. Decide which verbs you want pupils to practise – for example, common irregulars: *aller, être, avoir, faire* (to go, to be, to have, to do). Write a grid like this on the board:

	je	*tu*	*il*	*nous*	*vous*	*ils*
aller						
être						
avoir						
faire						

2. Divide the class into teams of six pupils. Tell pupils that everyone must pay attention, even if it is not their turn at the board, as it will help them when their turn does come.

3. The players from Team A each pick up a board pen and line up, one under each of the personal pronouns. Tell them they have two minutes to complete the grid.

4. Say *'Partez !'* ('Go!') and start the countdown. All six pupils must write the form of the first verb that corresponds to the pronoun they are standing under. For example, the first pupil on the left writes *vais* in the grid.

5. Then they all shift to the right, and the last player on the right runs to the left of the grid. They repeat step 4 with the second, third and fourth verbs.

6. At the end of two minutes (or whatever time works for your class), say *'Arrêtez !'* ('Stop!'). Count the number of correct verb forms. The team scores as many points as they have correct forms. Quickly correct any mistakes and then rub out all the verb forms, leaving an empty grid.

7. The next team lines up. As they were watching the first team and learning from their mistakes, reduce their time limit to 1 minute 50 seconds. The third team gets 1 minute 40 seconds, etc. The team with most points at the end wins.

Useful phrases

Mettez-vous en groupes de six.	Make up groups of six.
Complétez les verbes dans la grille.	Complete the verb forms in the grid.
Déplacez-vous vers la droite.	Move to your right.

Comments

- You can adapt this game to practise other grammar points; for example, adjectival agreements.

	m. sg.	*f. sg.*	*m. pl.*	*f. pl.*
grand				
petit				
beau				
blanc				

 This activity can be done by pupils individually. To increase the challenge, change the order of the personal pronouns in the grid, to *elles/je/vous/tu/nous/ elle*, for example.

Notes

....

....

....

....

....

....

....

....

....

....

....

....

11   Guess the verbs/*Verbes mimés*

Step by step

Classroom management	Whole class/teams
Skill	Grammar (writing)
Aim	To practise conjugating verbs
Resources	Word cards

1. In advance, prepare a number of cards with the infinitive form of verbs pupils are familiar with, and which are easy to mime. For example, for verbs ending in *-er*: *marcher, jouer, regarder, écouter, chanter, danser, parler, téléphoner* (to walk, to play, to look, to listen, to sing, to dance, to speak, to phone).

2. Divide the class into teams. One pupil from each team comes to the board.

3. Give each team a card. Nobody is allowed to speak. Team members read the card (e.g. *marcher)* and mime the verb (walking) until their teammate at the board writes it correctly in the infinitive form.

4. Each team must then complete the rest of the conjugation, one pupil at a time, so Pupil 1 comes to the board and writes *je marche*, Pupil 2 writes *tu marches*, etc.

5. When they have written out all parts of the verb, they hand the card back to you and collect a new verb card. A different pupil goes to the front. Repeat the process. Each verb correctly guessed and conjugated is worth a point.

6. The team with the most points at the end of the game wins.

Useful phrases

Lisez la carte.	Read the card.
Mimez le verbe.	Mime the verb.
Écris l'infinitif du verbe.	Write the verb in the infinitive [to a single pupil].
Venez écrire les autres formes du verbe.	Come up and write the other verb forms.

Comments

•   You could use a timer so that it becomes a race against the clock and pupils have to speed up.

Increase the level of challenge by mixing the verbs (e.g. regular verbs ending in *-er, -ir*) as well as common irregular verbs (such as *être, avoir, aller, faire*).

Add a few regular verbs which pupils might not have come across, and see if they can apply the spelling rules they have met to conjugate them anyway.

12 String ensemble/*La ficelle*

Step by step

The aim of this game is for pupils to conjugate as many verbs as possible (with pronouns they are familiar with) in a given time.

Classroom management	Whole class/teams
Skill	Grammar (speaking)
Aim	To practise conjugating verbs
Resources	A ball of string Timer/stopwatch

1. Write or display the pronouns your pupils know (*je, tu, il/elle/on, nous, vous, ils/elles*) and a list of verbs in the infinitive form on the board. For example: *être, aller, parler, aimer,* (to be, to go, to speak, to love).

2. Divide the class into two teams. Team A sits in a circle. Give the team a ball of string.

3. Start the timer. The first pupil holds the end of the string and starts to conjugate a verb from the board (i.e. says the *je* form) and then throws the ball to the person on their right. She continues the same verb (i.e. says the *tu* form) before throwing the ball of string to the person on her right, and so on. For example, for the verb *être* (to be):

   P1: *Je suis*

   P2: *Tu es*

   P3: *Il est* etc.

4. If a pupil makes a mistake, cannot say the right form of the verb or drops the ball of string, the ball must be rewound before it is passed on.

5. At the end of a given time, cut the length of string used by Team A. Repeat the process from step 3 with Team B. (Make sure the distance between the first and last pupil in each team is the same.)

6. Compare the two pieces of string. The team with the longest wins.

> **Useful phrases**

Conjuguez les verbes au tableau.	Conjugate the verbs listed on the board.
Tiens le bout de la ficelle.	Hold on to the start of the string [to a single pupil].
Passe la pelote à ton voisin/ ta voisine.	Throw the ball of string to the pupil next to you [to a single pupil].
Il faut rembobiner la ficelle.	Wind up the string.

Comments

- To keep pupils from Team B active and engaged while Team A is playing, tell them they must listen very carefully as, if they can spot an error, they can ask you to pause the timer and make a challenge which, if correct, could result in the string being rewound.

 To increase the level of difficulty, challenge pupils *not* to conjugate the verbs in the usual order (*je, tu, il,* etc.) but in a random order (*il, nous, je, elles*). The team must listen carefully at all times since, if one of them repeats a pronoun previously used for the same verb, you could ask them to rewind the string.

Notes

13 Family feud/*Les uns contre les autres*

Step by step

1. Decide which grammar point you want pupils to practise. This game works well for present-tense conjugations of regular verbs and common irregular verbs.

2. Divide the class into two 'families'. They could give themselves a French name, e.g. *les Durand* and *les Martin* (the top two surnames in France).

Classroom management	Whole class/teams
Skill	Grammar (reading, speaking or writing)
Aim	To practise any grammar point (e.g. present-tense verb conjugations)
Resources	None

3. One player from each 'family' comes to the board. Write or display a verb in English on the board. For example, if working on conjugations, write: 'I eat' or 'You (sing.) play' or 'She walks' etc.

4. The first of the two players to put up their hand and say the French equivalent gets two points if they answer correctly. If they make a mistake, the other player has a go at answering. If he too makes a mistake, his teammates can put up their hands and give the answer. Give one point for a correct answer given by teammates.

5. Another pupil from each team comes to the board for the next round. Continue until all team members have had a go.

6. The team with most points at the end of the game wins.

Useful phrases

Séparez-vous en deux familles.	Divide yourselves into two families.
Donnez-vous un nom.	Give yourselves a name.
Une personne de chaque famille vient au tableau.	One person from each family comes to the board.
Levez la main pour répondre.	Put up your hand to answer.

Comments

- A variation is to ask the pupils at the front to write their answers on the board rather than respond orally.

To increase the level of challenge, and for pupils to earn an extra point, ask them to use the word in a sentence.

14 The dot game/*Le jeu des carrés*

Step by step

1. Decide on a grammar point you want your pupils to practise, for example, the French words for 'my' (*mon/ma/mes*). Prepare a list of nouns, making sure there is a variety of masculine, feminine and plural.

2. Draw twenty-five dots in a square on the board (five across and five down – see below).

Classroom management	Whole class/teams
Skill	Grammar (speaking)
Aim	To practise any grammar points (e.g. possessive adjectives)
Resources	None

3. Divide the class into two teams, A and B. One pupil from Team A comes to the board. You say a noun; she repeats it with the correct possessive adjective. For example:

    T: *Le chien* (the dog).

    P1: *Mon chien* (my dog).

4. If she answers correctly, she can draw a horizontal or a vertical line from one of the dots to another. Another pupil from Team A comes to the board and does the same. The aim is to make up a square which the team can claim by writing A or B in its centre.

5. When a pupil answers incorrectly, the game goes to the other team. When all the lines have been drawn in, the team with the most squares on the board is the winner.

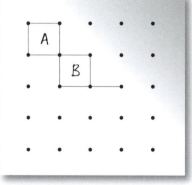

 Useful phrases

Pour une bonne réponse, tire un trait.   If you answer correctly, draw a line.

Quand tu as quatre lignes, tu gagnes le carré.   When you have four lines, you win the square.

Qui a le plus de carrés?   Who has the greatest number of squares?

Comments

• This game can be used to practise any grammar point.

 To increase the challenge, impose a time limit (e.g. a maximum of three seconds to respond).

15 Battleships/*La bataille navale*

Step by step

In case pupils are not familiar with the game of Battleships, explain that each player is given a card that contains two grids, one on which to place his ships (here, on one square only), the other on which to mark the position of his partner's ships. A player calls out some coordinates, for instance column 1, row F.

Classroom management	Pair-work
Skill	Grammar (writing, listening and speaking)
Aim	To practise any grammar point (e.g. conjugations)
Resources	Battleships grids

If the other player has a ship positioned at the intersection, she must say 'Hit'; if not, she says 'Miss'. The first pupil to sink the other person's fleet wins.

1. Prepare and photocopy grammar battleship grids in advance.

   For example, use the grids below to practise the verbs to eat, to play, to dance, to sing, to jump and the pronouns he/we/they/I/you(singular)/you (plural).

	il	*nous*	*ils*	*je/j'*	*tu*	*vous*
manger						
jouer						
danser						
chanter						
sauter						

2. Pupils decide where to hide eight 'ships'. In this instance, the 'ships' are actually the correct present-tense verb forms which pupils write in the appropriate squares. Check that they have conjugated all the verbs correctly before the start of the game. For example:

	il	*nous*	*ils*	*je/'j'*	*tu*	*vous*
aimer			*aiment*		*aimes*	
jouer	*joue*					
danser		*dansons*		*danse*		
chanter						*chantez*
sauter	*saute*		*sautent*			

3. Pupil 1 starts. He uses the coordinates (across and up/down, here the pronoun and the infinitive of the verb, which he must conjugate and spell correctly to match the pronoun).

For example:

P1: *'Nous jouons'* (we play).

P2: *Raté !* (Miss!) *À moi: 'Nous dansons'* (My turn: we dance).

P1: *Coulé !* (Hit!)

Both pupils note if it is a hit or a miss on the appropriate square on their grids. When a pupil scores a hit, he can have another go.

4. They continue to play until they sink all the other player's 'ships' or until time runs out (in that case, count the number of hits to decide the winner).

 Useful phrases

Complétez huit cases de votre grille.	Complete eight squares on your grid.
Choisissez un sujet, je, tu, il, etc.	Choose a subject (*je, tu, il,* etc.).
Donnez la bonne forme du verbe.	Say the correct form of the verb.

Comments

- This game can be adapted to practise a wide variety of grammar points, for instance conjugations of irregular verbs, conjugations of verbs in different tenses, adjectival agreements, position of adjectives, etc.

- For adjective agreements, you could draw up a grid like this to practise a dog/a cat/a fish/a hamster/a rabbit and the adjectives white/small/red/big/tall/black.

	blanc	*petit*	*rouge*	*gros*	*grand*	*noir*
un chien						
un chat						
un poisson						
un hamster						
un lapin						

- If you have not been able to photocopy grids in advance, write one on the board for pupils to copy twice on a sheet of paper.

Increase the challenge by asking pupils to use the words in the grid in a sentence.

16 Ping-pong/*Ping-pong*

Step by step

1. Decide on a grammar point you want pupils to practise, for example, using the negative *(ne ... pas)*.

2. Divide the class into two teams, A and B, and get them to line up.

3. One pupil from each team comes to the board. Pupil 1 from Team A starts by saying a sentence, either positive or negative. Pupil 1 from Team B must automatically say the opposite. For example:

Classroom management	Whole class/teams or groups of three
Skill	Grammar (listening and speaking)
Aim	To practise any grammar points (e.g. negative phrases)
Resources	Optional: ping-pong ball

P1 A: *J'aime le chocolat* (I like chocolate).

P1 B: *Moi, je n'aime pas le chocolat* (Me, I don't like chocolate).

4. If Pupil 1 from Team B gets it right, he then gets the 'ball' and 'throws' a sentence at his opponent. If she doesn't get it right, she goes to the end of the line and is replaced by another pupil. For her team to keep the ball, another pupil from the team can answer. If no one in the team can answer, Team B gets the ball and says a sentence. Repeat until all pupils have had a go.

5. If the first sentence of a set is wrong, you need to stop the game and call a fault, as you would in a game of ping-pong. The pupil can either correct his sentence or get a member of the team to help. If no one in the team can help, that pupil is replaced by another and the other team takes the ball.

> **Useful phrases**

Deux élèves au tableau.	Two pupils come to the board.
Élève 1 dit une phrase.	Pupil 1 says a sentence.
Élève 2 dit (le contraire).	Pupil 2 says (the opposite).
Tu vas en queue de file.	You go to the back of the line.

Comments

- The principle of this game can be used for a wide range of grammatical points. It works especially well for oppositions such as masculine/feminine adjectives (*petit/petite, grand/grande, vert/verte*, etc.), singular/irregular plurals (*un animal/des animaux*, etc.), and also with verbs (conjugations: different forms, e.g. *je suis/tu es; j'ai/tu as; il est/elle est; nous allons/vous allez*, or different tenses, e.g. *je mange/j'ai mangé*).

- You could use a scorekeeper to keep track of the number of sentences each team says correctly.

- A variation is to play this game in groups of three, with one able pupil acting as umpire. Her role is to say when a player is making a mistake.

 To increase the challenge, eliminate pupils who do not reply within three or four seconds.

Pupils could throw an actual ping-pong ball when saying their sentence – their opponent has to catch it as they reply.

Notes

....

....

....

....

....

....

....

....

....

....

....

....

....

....

....

....

17 Home base/*Chacun chez soi*

Step by step

Play this game once pupils understand the concept of gender in French and are familiar with the determiners *un/une* (a) and/or *le/la* (the).

Classroom management	Whole class/teams
Skill	Grammar (reading and speaking)
Aim	To practise any grammar points (e.g. gender)
Resources	Two large cards, smaller cards Optional: bell

1. Prepare two large cards in advance: one with the words *noms masculins* (masculine nouns) written on it, and the other with *noms féminins* (feminine nouns) written on it, as well as a set of small cards with French nouns on them, some masculine and some feminine, and a determiner *un/une* – and *le/la* if pupils are familiar with both. For example: *une pizza/un gâteau/la limonade/le café* (a pizza, a cake, the lemonade, the coffee).

2. Display the large cards, one on each side of the classroom (or hall, if possible, as children will have more space to move around).

3. Divide pupils into two teams. Give each pupil a small card with a determiner and noun on it. They then walk around and when you give the signal (ring a bell if you have one or clap your hands), they must rush to the correct card: *noms masculins* if they have a masculine noun on their card, and *noms féminins* if it's a feminine one.

4. In turn, pupils read their cards aloud to check if they're next to the correct large card. This gives you an opportunity to ensure they pronounce *un/une* and *le/la* correctly.

5. If they are correct, they come and give their cards back to you and score a point for their team. If they're not, they give you their cards but don't score.

6. Shuffle and redistribute the cards. Repeat the game from step 4. You can stop the game at any time. The team with most points wins.

Useful phrases

Lisez votre carte.	Read your card.
Au signal, courez vers le bon panneau.	On my signal, run to the correct large card.
Lisez votre carte tout haut.	Read out your card.

Comments

- You can adapt this game to practise different grammar points such as the notion of number, matching nouns/adjectives on the cards to the large cards saying *Singulier* (singular) or *Pluriel* (plural).

- You could also practise conjugations, especially tricky irregular verbs: prepare two large cards with, for example, '*Être*' (to be) and '*Avoir*' (to have), and give pupils cards with conjugated forms of both verbs: *ai, as, a, avons, avez, ont* (have/has) and *suis, es, est, sommes, êtes, sont* (am/are/is).

- For regular verbs ending in *-er* or *-ir* in the present tense, have six panels: *je, tu, il/elle/on, nous, vous, ils/elles*, and pupils should have cards with conjugated forms.

You can vary the level of challenge. For younger pupils, first practise determiners by making two large cards (*Masculin/Féminin*) along with smaller cards with the determiners: *un, une, le, la* (possibly *mon, ma*, etc.). They have to go to the relevant large card.

For more able pupils, make different cards with adjectives on them, some masculine, some feminine. Pupils must decide whether their adjective goes with a masculine or a feminine noun.

To make it even more challenging, increase the number of large cards, for example: *masculin singulier, masculin pluriel, féminin singulier, féminin pluriel*.

Notes

....

....

....

....

....

....

....

....

....

18 Treasure trail/*La course au trésor*

Step by step

1. Decide which grammar point(s) you want pupils to revise, such as negative sentences. Make a list of positive sentences that pupils will have to transform into negative ones. Vary the level of difficulty to suit your class. For example:

Classroom management	Whole class/teams
Skill	Grammar (listening and speaking)
Aim	To revise one or more grammar points (any type) e.g. negative phrases
Resources	List of positive sentences

   1. *Je suis anglais* (I'm English) (negative: *Je ne suis pas anglais*)
   2. *J'ai dix ans* (I'm ten) (negative: *Je n'ai pas dix ans*)
   3. *J'habite en France* (I live in France) (negative: *Je n'habite pas en France*)
   4. *J'aime le pain* (I like bread) (negative: *Je n'aime pas le pain*)
   5. *J'aime les chiens* (I like dogs) (negative: *Je n'aime pas les chiens*)
   6. *J'aime jouer au rugby* (I like playing rugby) (negative: *Je n'aime pas jouer au rugby*)

2. On the board, draw two treasure trails, one the mirror image of the other. Write '*Départ*' in the first square in each grid, and add two stars in random squares per grid. Explain to pupils that they can only ask for the help of their teammates when they are on a square with a star.

3. Divide the class into two teams. One pupil from each team comes to the board. Say the first sentence. Whoever puts their hand up first says the negative version of the sentence. If their sentence is correct, they put a cross in the square next to '*Départ*'. If the sentence is not correct, they don't move on the trail and the pupil from the other team gets a chance to answer. Again, if the answer is correct, they put a cross on their trail; if not, they stay put.

4. Both pupils go back to their teams and another two pupils come up to the board. Continue until one of the teams reaches the treasure.

5. Repeat the process, starting on another trail, until all pupils from both teams have come up to the board. The team who reaches the treasure first wins.

Useful phrases	*Levez la main pour répondre.*	Put up your hand to give the answer.
	Le plus rapide répond.	The person who is fastest answers.
	Mets une croix dans la case.	Put a cross on the trail [to a single pupil].

Comments

- This is a good game to play at the end of term. You could give your grid a festive theme: for instance, make it an Easter treasure trail at Easter, adding a picture of an Easter rabbit in the *'Départ'* square and a couple of Easter eggs in two other squares. At Christmas, draw a Christmas tree and a couple of presents.

To increase the level of challenge, you could make longer trails, such as those shown below.

19 Hats off!/*Chapeau !*

Step by step

This is a game of concentration and memory as well as a good opportunity to revise grammar points. The aim is to go around a trail on the board, answering questions and grabbing as many hats as possible from your opponents.

Classroom management	Whole class/teams
Skill	Grammar (listening and speaking)
Aim	To revise one or more grammar points (any type)
Resources	List of sixteen questions Optional: sticky notes

1. In advance, prepare a list of sixteen questions, relating to any grammar point you want your pupils to revise, adapting the level to suit your class. For example:

   1. *Il est grand. Elle est ...?* (or What is the feminine form of the adjective *grand*?)
   2. *Je suis, tu es, il ou elle ...* (or What part of '*être*' goes with '*il*' or '*elle*' (singular)?)
   3. Do you say *Je joue à le football* or *je joue* au *football ?* (or What preposition is needed in this sentence? *Je joue ... football),* etc.

2. On the board, draw or display a trail with sixteen circles numbered 1 to 16.

3. Divide the class into four teams. Each team chooses a colour and/or a name. Write the team names in different colours on the board. Draw two top hats by each team. Draw a token in the colour of the team (or, better, as it avoids having to draw them and rub them off, place sticky notes with a blob of colour for each team) at regular intervals on the game board (e.g. blue on number 1, green on number 5, red on number 9, yellow on number 13).

Explain to pupils that as long as they can answer a question, they can move their token clockwise one circle at a time. If they overtake an opponent on the board, they

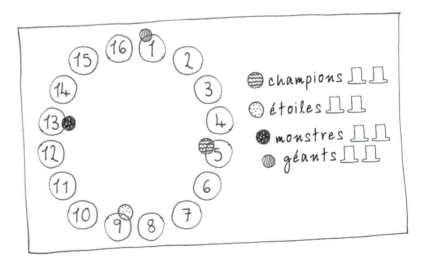

can grab one of their hats (in which case you rub it off on the board and redraw it by the team that grabbed it).

4. Start the game with Team A on circle 1. Ask them question number 2 so that they can move forward. Pupils in that team can discuss quietly before one pupil gives the answer. If it is correct, move the token to circle 2 and ask them question 3. (You may decide to ask a maximum number of questions, e.g. four, in any one go.)

If they can't answer or answer incorrectly, it is another team's turn. Team B starts on circle 5. Ask them question number 6.

Point out that they need to really concentrate and try to remember the other team's answers as they will all have to answer every question eventually. The more they can answer correctly the first time, the faster they can go round the trail to build up their collection of hats. And it's hats off to the winning team (the team with most hats)!

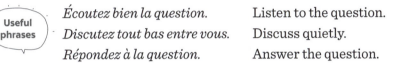

Useful phrases	*Écoutez bien la question.*	Listen to the question.
	Discutez tout bas entre vous.	Discuss quietly.
	Répondez à la question.	Answer the question.

Comments

- This game can suit any language point, vocabulary, pronunciation, etc.
- You could include some writing by asking pupils to come to the board and write the answer. Check it to make sure it's correct, or correct it if necessary, and then rub it off.

To increase the level of challenge, only one pupil in each team can answer the question and her teammates must not help her. To show whose turn it is to speak, ask team members to take turns to hold a specific object (a soft toy, a ruler, a pencil case, etc.). The pupil holding the object answers, then passes the object to the person sitting next to him. He will be the person answering the next question.

Notes

....

....

....

....

....

20 Sentence auction/*Phrases aux enchères*

Step by step

The aim of this game is to spot and correct mistakes in sentences.

Classroom management	Groups
Skill	Grammar (reading, speaking)
Aim	To revise any grammar point
Resources	List of questions

1. In advance, prepare a number of sentences, some correct, some with deliberate mistakes. Use language you have previously covered in class.

2. Divide the class into small groups.

3. Explain the principle of the 'auction': each group has €30 to spend. The aim is to 'buy' correct sentences. A bid begins at €1 and each subsequent bid increases by €1 or more. Groups must try to outbid each other. The sentence will be sold to the highest bidder. The group who has bought the greatest number of correct sentences wins.

4. Revise numbers 1 to 30 with the class (see the Number games on pages 145–171).

5. Write the name of each group on the board and the total amount of money they have (€30). Keep a tally of the money each group spends (you could nominate pupils to do this).

6. Write eight sentences on the board, for example (errors are underlined):
    1. *Je suis anglais* (I'm English).
    2. *Je s'appelle Paul (Je m'appelle Paul)* (My name is Paul).
    3. *Je suis six ans (J'ai six ans)* (I'm six years old).
    4. *Je habite à Londres (J'habite à Londres)* (I live in London).
    5. *Je joue au football* (I play football).
    6. *Mon anniversaire, c'est en mai* (My birthday's in May).
    7. *J'est un chien (J'ai un chien)* (I have a dog).
    8. *Mon chien est noir* (My dog is black).

7. Ask who wants to start the bidding for the first sentence for €1. When groups stop bidding, say the traditional 'Going once. Going twice. Sold' (*Une fois, deux fois, trois fois ... adjugé, vendu !*).

    T: *La phrase numéro 1, un euro.*

    Group A: *Un euro !*

    Group B: *Deux euros !*

    Group C: *Cinq euros ... etc.*

    T: *Une fois, deux fois, trois fois ... adjugé, vendu ! Phrase numéro 1 à l'équipe C pour cinq euros !*

8. Once the game has finished, go through each sentence asking the class whether it is correct or incorrect. If the sentence is correct, the team that bought it gets one point. If the sentence is incorrect, no points are awarded. For a bonus point, ask who can explain why it is incorrect. The team with most points wins.

Useful phrases	*La phrase numéro X pour Y euros.*	Sentence number *X* for *Y* euros.
	Qui dit mieux !	Any advance on ...?
	Une fois, deux fois ... adjugé, vendu !	Going once. Going twice. Sold!

Comments

*   If a group runs out of money early in the auction, you could let them buy some money from the bank (i.e. you) by getting them to do something in French, such as translate a word/a phrase, etc. If no one wants to buy a sentence because they spot an obvious mistake, give a bonus point to the team that can correct it.

To vary the level of challenge, play 'Word auction' with younger pupils, and check the spelling of individual words.

Notes

....

....

....

....

....

....

....

....

....

....

Part 7: Playing with sounds

Good pronunciation is not always easy when the sounds of the foreign language are different from your own. But with plenty of practice, it's possible to master new sounds and intonation patterns, and children can have fun recognising and imitating them.

In the games in this part of the book, pupils have the chance to:

* listen and identify sounds
* distinguish various sounds
* repeat and produce the sounds
* link the written form to the sound it represents (grapheme to phoneme).

Appendix 1 is a handy reference list of all the sounds in French (see page 243) and Appendix 2 includes a list of short rhymes, each focusing on a different sound (see page 245).

Many of the games from other parts of this book can be adapted to practise sounds too, such as:

Part 2: Speaking – games 1, 3, 4, 5, 7, 13

Part 4: Writing – games 1, 2, 4, 12, 14, 16

Part 6: Grammar – games 1, 7, 8, 16, 17.

And if you are in need of a quick and easy 'sounds' activity, tongue-twisters are ideal (see activity 18 on page 238). There's a list on page 248 to get you started.

1   Sound tower/*La tour des sons*

Step by step

1. Decide which sound you are going to introduce (see page 243) and prepare a list of words, some which contain that sound and others which don't. For example, to focus on the sound 'on': *bonbon, chanson, chaussette, poisson, ananas, maison, pantalon, éléphant, lion, cousin, cousine, tante, oncle* (sweet, song, sock, fish, pineapple, house, trousers, elephant, lion, male cousin, female cousin, aunt, uncle).

Classroom management	Whole class/pairs/small groups
Skill	Sounds
Aim	To listen for and identify a specific sound
Resources	A list of words (or text) Multilink cubes

2. Divide the class into pairs or small groups and distribute multilink cubes (or other props that can be piled on top of each other) to each.

3. Read out the words once. Pupils listen. Then read them out again. This time, pupils grab a cube each time they hear the sound.

4. At the end, they build a tower and count how many cubes they have.

5. Read out the words again and count up the number of times the sound you are focusing on appears. Pupils unclick a multilink cube each time the sound appears. The winning pairs/groups are those whose tower has the exact number of cubes.

> **Useful phrases**
>
> | | |
> |---|---|
> | *Écoutez les mots.* | Listen to the words. |
> | *Prenez un cube quand vous entendez le son « on ».* | Grab a cube when you hear the sound 'on'. |
> | *Construisez une tour !* | Build a tower! |
> | *Il y a combien de cubes dans votre tour ?* | How many cubes are there in your tower? |

Comments

- For more difficult sounds (e.g. 'é'/'ai' or 'u'/'ou'), before playing the game, read out the words several times and ask pupils to put up their hand or do a mime every time they hear the sound you are focusing on.

- You could make up a specific mime for each of the sounds you introduce and practise: right hand on forehead pointing down for é and left hand on forehead pointing down for è.

To make it a bit more challenging, pupils could play on their own, rather than in pairs or groups.

To increase the level of linguistic challenge, find a short text (e.g. a poem, story or song) containing lots of examples of the sound you are focusing on.

Notes

....

....

....

....

....

....

....

....

....

....

....

....

....

....

....

....

....

....

2   All together/*Tous ensemble*

Step by step

1. Decide which sound you are going to introduce (see page 243) and prepare a list of words or short phrases, some containing that sound and others that don't. For example, to focus on the sound '*é*': *le café, le boulanger, la piscine, le musée, ma tête, mon nez, un bras, deux pieds* (the café, the bakery,

Classroom management	Whole class
Skill	Sounds
Aim	To listen to and identify a specific sound
Resources	A list of words

   the swimming pool, the museum, my head, my nose, an arm, two feet).

2. Divide the class into groups.

3. Read out the words. When pupils hear the sound they are focusing on, they must stand up at once. If any pupil in a group doesn't stand up, or stands up when he shouldn't, the whole group gets a penalty point.

4. The winning group is the group with the fewest penalty points once all the words have been read out.

> **Useful phrases**
>
> *Mettez-vous en groupes de (quatre).* — Make up groups of (four).
>
> *Écoutez et repérez le son « é ».* — Listen carefully for the sound 'é'.
>
> *Quand vous entendez « é », levez-vous ensemble !* — When you hear 'é', stand up all together!
>
> *Vous avez un gage !* — You have a penalty point!

Comments

- As listening practice for sounds that pupils are already familiar with, read a longer text (e.g. a poem, story or song) containing lots of examples of the sounds you are focusing on, and give each group a different sound to listen out for.

To increase the challenge, choose words that contain similar sounds. For example, if you are practising 'u' or 'ou', use words such as *dessus, dessous, le pull, la poule* (above, below, the sweater, the hen).

3 Right hand, left hand/ *Main droite, main gauche*

Step by step

1. Decide which two sounds you want pupils to recognise (from the list on page 243). For example, you could focus on the sounds 'on' and 'en'.

2. Prepare a list of words with both the 'on' sound and the 'en' sound. For example: *marron, marrant, orange, rond, charmant, géant, mignon, amusant, prénom, dents, décontracté* (brown, funny, orange, round, charming, giant, cute, fun, first name, teeth, casual).

Classroom management	Whole class
Skill	Sounds
Aim	To distinguish between sounds
Resources	A list of words (or text)

3. Decide with the class which hand represents the 'on' sound and which the 'en' sound.

4. Tell pupils they each have nine lives in this game. Start reading the words from the list. For each word, pupils put up either their right or their left hand, depending on the sound they hear.

5. When a pupil gets it wrong, she loses one of her nine lives (or you could choose a smaller number if you want to make it more competitive). The winner is the one with most lives left at the end of the game.

> **Useful phrases**
>
> *Écoutez les mots.* — Listen to the words.
> *Pour le son « X », levez la main droite.* — When you hear 'X', put up your right hand.
> *Pour le son « Y », levez la main gauche.* — When you hear 'Y', put up your left hand.

Comments

- You could add a speaking element to this game by asking pupils to say the words, reproducing the sound as accurately as possible. If they do so correctly, they can stay in the game.

 To increase the challenge, read aloud a poem or a short story with words containing the sounds in focus. Pupils put up their hands when they hear the sounds.

4 Loudspeakers/*Haut-parleurs*

Step by step

1. Decide which two sounds you are going to practise (see page 243), such as *'ye'* (as in *vanille* (vanilla)) or *'gn'* (as in *montagne* (mountain)) and prepare a list of short phrases that contain one of the sounds, but not both. For example: *une glace à la vanille ; une maison à la montagne ; j'ai mal à l'œil ; un weekend à la campagne ; voici ma famille ; j'aime les champignons ; sur le pont d'Avignon ; c'est quelle taille ?* (a vanilla ice cream; a house in the mountains; I have a sore eye; a weekend in the country; this is my family; I like mushrooms; on the bridge at Avignon; what size is it?).

Classroom management	Whole class
Skill	Sounds
Aim	To distinguish between sounds
Resources	A list of phrases

2. Choose two pupils to act as *'haut-parleurs'* (loudspeakers) and give each one a sound to repeat. Make sure they can both say their sound correctly. One goes to one side of the classroom or hall, and the other to the other side.

3. Tell pupils they each have nine lives in this game. Start reading aloud your list of words. The two loudspeakers say their sound and pupils must point to the appropriate one. For example:

   T: *Numéro 1 = une glace à la vanille.* Pupils point to the pupil saying « *ye, ye, ye* ». If they don't, they lose one of their nine lives (or you could choose a smaller number if you want to make it more competitive).

4. Repeat the process until you have read all the words on your list.

Écoutez bien les mots.	Listen to the words carefully.
Montrez le bon haut-parleur.	Point to the right loudspeaker.
Tu es éliminé(e) !	You're out!

Comments

• It doesn't matter if the language you use is not all known to the pupils, as the focus here is purely on listening for a specific sound, not on understanding the phrases.

• A variation of this game which you could play outdoors or in a hall is Sound magnets (*L'attrape-sons*). Proceed as above but instead of pointing to the 'loudspeaker', pupils run to him. To speed up the game, give a time limit for pupils to get to the loudspeakers. Give a signal – clap your hands, blow a whistle or ring a bell – to show that time is up. Pupils who ran to the wrong loudspeaker or didn't reach one in time are eliminated. They are not out of the game but instead, they stand alongside one of the loudspeakers and join in making the sound with her. The winner is the last pupil who has not turned into a loudspeaker.

To increase the level of linguistic challenge, focus on three or four different sounds.

For more advanced classes, you could choose sounds that are harder to distinguish. For example, 'i', 'ai', 'é' and 'e' or 'ou', 'u', 'an' and 'on'.

Notes

....

....

....

....

....

....

....

....

....

....

....

....

....

....

....

5 Follow my leader/*Pigeon vole*

Step by step

1. Decide which sound you are going to introduce (see page 243). For example, you might choose the vowel sound 'i' or the consonant sound 'ch'. Prepare a list of words or short phrases, some which contain that sound and others which don't. For example,

Classroom management	Whole class
Skill	Sounds
Aim	To distinguish between sounds
Resources	A list of words

- for 'i': *un céleri, un avocat, une cerise, une poire, une fraise, un abricot, du raisin, une orange, une olive* (celery, an avocado, a cherry, a pear, a strawberry, an apricot, grapes, an orange, an olive).
- for 'ch': *un chou, une saucisse, un champignon, une framboise, un cornichon, du chocolat, une orange, une sardine* (a cabbage, a sausage, a mushroom, a raspberry, a gherkin, chocolate, an orange, a sardine).

2. Tell pupils they each have nine lives in this game. Start reading aloud the list. After each item, add '*vole*' and flap your arms.

   T: *Un céleri vole !* [flap your arms]. If the word you say contains the sound in focus, pupils copy you and raise their arms. When it doesn't contain the sound, you still flap your arms, but pupils must not move their arms. If they flap their arms by mistake, they're out or they lose one of their nine lives (or you could choose a smaller number if you want to make it more competitive).

   The winner is the last pupil remaining in the game.

> **Useful phrases**
>
> | | |
> |---|---|
> | *Écoutez bien.* | Listen carefully. |
> | *Le mot a le son « X ».* | The word has the sound 'X'. |
> | *Levez les bras !* | Raise your arms! |
> | *Le mot n'a pas de son « X».* | The word doesn't have the sound 'X'. |
> | *Ne levez pas les bras.* | Don't raise your arms. |
> | *Tu es éliminé(e) !* | You're out! |

Comments

- This game is based on a traditional French playground game called *Pigeon vole* (literally, 'pigeon flies', roughly equivalent to the British game of Follow my leader).

- More advanced pupils could also play the game in groups, with one pupil taking on the role of leader and reading the words, or in pairs, taking turns at reading the list of words aloud.

 Increase the challenge by asking pupils to indicate in which syllable they hear the sound in focus by holding up the relevant number of fingers. For example, if you're focusing on the sound 'i', pupils hold up three fingers for the word *céleri*.

Notes

6 Sound tennis/*Le tennis des sons*

Step by step

Classroom management	Whole class
Skill	Sounds
Aim	To listen and produce sounds accurately
Resources	List of words Tennis ball (or soft toy)

1. Decide which sound you are going to introduce (see page 243) and prepare a list of words that contain that sound. For example, to focus on the sound 'qu' (pronounced 'k'), you could use: *quatre, quatorze, quarante, quand, quartier, quel, qui, queue, Québec, quinze, Turquie, équipe, requin* (four, fourteen, forty, when, neighbourhood, what, who, tail, Quebec, fifteen, Turkey, team, shark).

2. Explain that this is a 'Beat the teacher' game so the class will be playing against you.

3. As you call out a word from your list, throw a tennis ball to a pupil. She must catch the ball and repeat the word as accurately as possible. She must repeat the word again while throwing the ball back to you. If her pronunciation is good, the class scores a point.

4. If the pupil doesn't catch the ball, she gets a forfeit (e.g. she has to say the word five times) and you get a point.

5. If a pupil doesn't repeat a word accurately, the class must help him until he does if they don't want to lose a point.

> **Useful phrases**
>
> | | |
> |---|---|
> | *Écoutez et répétez le mot.* | Listen and repeat the word. |
> | *Attrapez la balle.* | Catch the ball. |
> | *Lancez la balle.* | Throw the ball. |
> | *Tu as un gage !* | You have a forfeit [to a single pupil]! |
> | *Répète le mot cinq fois.* | Repeat the word five times [to a single pupil]. |
> | *Un point pour moi/vous.* | A point for me/you. |

Comments

- A variation for younger pupils is Flying teddy (*Le nounours volant*), in which you replace the tennis ball with a soft toy.

 To increase the challenge, have pupils throw the tennis ball (or teddy) to another pupil instead of back to you. They must call out the word, making sure they pronounce it accurately.

7 King (or Queen) Parrot/*Le roi (ou La reine) des perroquets*

Step by step

The aim of this game is to provide pupils with the opportunity to learn and practise short phonetic French rhymes in a fun way.

Classroom management	Whole class
Skill	Sounds
Aim	To listen and produce sounds accurately
Resources	Easy French rhymes

1. Choose a French rhyme with a particular sound (see page 245). For example, you could focus on the sound 'oi' using this simple counting rhyme: *Une oie, deux oies, trois oies, quatre oies, cinq oies, six oies, c'est toi !* (*une oie* is a goose).

2. Tell pupils you are King (or Queen) Parrot and that they must copy exactly what you say and do. Go through the rhyme with the whole class several times using choral repetition, associating a gesture or a mime with each line. For example:

   T: *Une oie* [show a thumb].

   Class: *Une oie* [showing their thumbs].

   T: *Deux oies* [show one finger and thumb].

   Class: *Deux oies* [showing one finger and thumb]. (Then carry on with *trois oies, quatre oies, cinq oies, six oies* [showing the appropriate number of fingers each time].)

   T: *C'est toi !* (It's you!) [point at someone with your finger]. (Playing on the words *c'est toi*: sounding like *sept oies.*)

3. Once pupils are familiar with the rhyme, divide the class into teams.

4. Each team takes a turn at saying the rhyme using the appropriate gestures, without any prompt from you. Set a time limit, say two minutes, and see how many times the team can chorus the rhyme, using the correct pronunciation. If a team gets it wrong, it must start the rhyme from the beginning again. The team that says the whole rhyme accurately the most times is the winner.

Useful phrases

Je suis le roi des perroquets !   I'm King Parrot!

Faites comme moi.   Copy me.

Comments

- You could let more advanced pupils take on the role of King or Queen Parrot, adopting a special voice or style which the class has to copy.

 Increase the level of challenge by asking pupils to say the rhyme more and more quickly.

8   Sound hunt/*La chasse aux sons*

Step by step

1. Decide which sound you want pupils to practise (see page 243) and prepare a list of words, some which contain that sound and others which don't. For example, to focus on the sound 'ou', you could use: *une mouche, un oiseau, un loup, un mouton, un ours, un dauphin, une fourmi, un chien, une vache, un cochon, une baleine, un éléphant* (a fly, a bird, a wolf, a sheep, a bear, a dolphin, an ant, a dog, a cow, a pig, a whale, an elephant).

Classroom management	Whole class/groups
Skill	Sounds
Aim	To listen and produce sounds accurately
Resources	A list of words

2. Divide the class into two groups: the foxes and the hunters (about five or six pupils per group).

3. Give each fox a word from your list. Make sure they can pronounce the word accurately.

4. To start the game, call out an instruction to the hunters:

   T: *Chasseurs, chassez les mots avec le son « ou »* (Hunters, hunt for words with the sound 'ou').

5. The foxes say their words aloud while walking around the classroom. The hunters must listen carefully and spot a fox that is saying a word which contains the correct sound. They place a hand on the fox's arm or shoulder to indicate they have been caught. They go as a pair to see you to check.

6. If a hunter has caught a fox with the right sound, the fox becomes a hunter. If a hunter has caught a fox with the wrong sound, he must release the fox.

7. Repeat the same procedure with a different sound. The winners are the group (hunters or foxes) with the most pupils after a given time.

Useful phrases

Qui veut être chasseur ?	Who wants to be a hunter?
Répétez les mots.	Repeat the words.
Écoutez bien les renards.	Listen carefully to the foxes.
Attrapez les sons « ou ».	Catch the sound 'ou'.
Tu deviens chasseur.	You turn into a hunter [to a single pupil].

Comments

- This game is better played in a hall where pupils can speak loudly and move around freely.

 Increase the challenge by selecting sounds that are harder to distinguish. For example, 'i', 'ai', 'é' and 'e' or 'ou', 'u', 'an' and 'in'.

Notes

9 In town/*Dans la ville*

Step by step

1. This game is best suited to more
   advanced classes. The aim is for
   pupils to work out which sound you
   have secretly chosen to focus on for
   your town. For example, if you have
   chosen the sound 'en'/'an', ask the
   class:

Classroom management	Whole class
Skill	Sounds
Aim	To produce sounds accurately
Resources	None

   T: *Qu'est-ce qu'il y a dans ma ville ?* (What is there in my town?)

2. Pupils take turns suggesting things that could be in your town. If the word they say has your
   chosen sound, you say *oui* and give a thumbs-up. If the name they suggest does not contain
   that sound, say *non* and give a thumbs-down.

   For example:

   P1: *Dans la ville, il y a des maisons ?* (Are there houses in the town?)

   T: *Non.*

   P2: *Dans la ville, il y a des appartements ?* (Are there flats in the town?)

   T: *Oui.*

   P3: *Dans la ville, il y a des magasins ?* (Are there shops in the town?)

   T: *Non,* etc.

3. Keep going until one pupil works out what your sound is. She is the winner. Then start
   another round with a different sound.

Useful phrases

Écoutez ma question.	Listen to my question.
Faites des suggestions.	Make suggestions.
Quel est le son secret ?	What is the secret sound?

Comments

- A variation of this game is based on the traditional French game: *Au marché de Padipado*
  (The market of no 'i' and no 'o'), in which nothing with the sounds 'i' or 'o' is sold. Questions
  might be:

  P: *Au marché de Padipado, on vend des bananes ?* (Do they sell bananas in Padipado market?)

  T: *Oui.*

  P: *Au marché de Padipado, on vend des cerises ?* (Do they sell cherries in Padipado market?)

  T: *Non.*

Adapt the idea to practise other vocabulary and other sounds. For example: *Le zoo de Padupadou* (The zoo of no 'u' and no 'ou'), *Le magasin de Padapadé* (The shop of no 'a' and no 'é'), etc.

You could suggest a sound to a few able pupils without the rest of the class hearing. Each one could then work with a small group of pupils, answering their questions as above.

Notes

....

....

....

....

....

....

....

....

....

....

....

....

....

....

10 Great Mamamouchi/*Le grand Mamamouchi*

Step by step

The aim of this game is similar to game 9 but it offers the opportunity for a bit of drama as pupils act out roles of *le grand Mamamouchi* and his obsequious courtiers!

Classroom management	Whole class
Skill	Sounds
Aim	To produce sounds accurately
Resources	None

1. Choose a pupil, or ask a volunteer, to be *le grand Mamamouchi* (the whimsical king). Together, you secretly choose a sound, for example 'i', that you do not want to hear.

2. Explain to the rest of the class that they are courtiers bringing gifts to their king. He will accept some and refuse others, according to the sounds in the names of the gifts. They must work out which sound Mamamouchi has chosen.

   P1: *O! Grand Mamamouchi, j'apporte en cadeau ... un bijou* (Oh, great Mamamouchi, I bring you a jewel as a gift).

   P2 (Mamamouchi): *Ah non, pas question !* (Ah no, no way!)

   P3: *O! Grand Mamamouchi, j'apporte en cadeau ... des bonbons* (Oh, great Mamamouchi, I bring you sweets as a gift).

   P2 (Mamamouchi): *Ah oui, merci !* (Great, thank you).

3. The pupil who works out the forbidden sound becomes Mamamouchi next. Play the game again, focusing on a different sound this time.

> **Useful phrases**
>
> *Qui veut être le grand Mamamouchi ?*
> Who wants to be the great Mamamouchi?
>
> *Pensez à des cadeaux pour le grand Mamamouchi.*
> Think of gifts to bring to the great Mamamouchi.
>
> *Le grand Mamamouchi n'aime pas les mots avec quel son ?*
> Which sound doesn't the great Mamamouchi like?

Comments

• Support younger pupils or beginners by providing them with a list of possible gifts, making sure there is a great variety of sounds in their names.

- Suggest older, more advanced pupils use a bilingual dictionary to find the vocabulary they would like to use. This provides a novel opportunity to ensure good sound–spelling links. For instance, *une armoire* (a wardrobe) contains a letter 'i' but not the sound 'i'.

 To add a memory challenge, at the end of the game, ask pupils if they can remember all the gifts refused by Mamamouchi and all those he accepted. Insist on accurate pronunciation.

Notes

....

....

....

....

....

....

....

....

....

....

....

....

....

....

....

....

11 Splat!/*Splaf !*

Step by step

1. Decide on the sound you want pupils to practise (see page 243). Prepare a list with words containing that sound and similar words with different sounds. For example, to focus on the sound 'e' and its various spellings, how about: *jeu, j'ai, joue, gens* (game, I've, play, people); *de, doux, dans, des* (of, soft, on, the); *nœud, nous, nez,*

Classroom management	Whole class
Skill	Sounds
Aim	To make accurate sound–spelling links
Resources	A list of words Two fly-swatters

nid (knot, we/us, nose, nest); *patte, petit, pâté, pêche* (paw, small, pâté, peach); *deux, dans, dent, daim* (two, on, tooth, deer). Write two words from your list on the board and say them aloud.

2. Divide the class into two teams. One pupil from each team comes to the board. If you have fly-swatters, give them one each.

3. Call out one of the words written on the board. The first pupil to splat it (with the swatter or with his hand) wins a point for his team. The pair return to their seats and are replaced by two more pupils.

4. Repeat several times until everyone has had a go. The team with the most points at the end of the game wins.

Useful phrases		
Faites deux équipes.	Divide into two teams.
Venez au tableau.	Come to the board.
Tapez sur le mot !	Splat the word!
Tu gagnes !	You win [to a single pupil]!

Comments

• You could add a speaking element to this game by asking pupils to say the words and reproduce the sound as accurately as possible before they sit down. If they do so, they win an extra point for their team.

Increase the level of challenge by writing more words on the board for pupils to choose from.

12 Odd one out/*Chassez l'intrus*

Step by step

Classroom management	Whole class
Skill	Sounds
Aim	To make accurate sound–spelling links
Resources	A list of words

1. Decide which sound you want pupils to practise (see page 243) and prepare a list of four words, three that contain that sound and one that doesn't. For example, to focus on the sound '*è*', how about: *frère, sœur, père, mère* (brother, sister, father, mother); *reine, prince, princesse, palais* (king, prince, princess, palace); *fête, chèvre, Noël, pâté* (celebration, goat, Christmas, pâté); *seize, sept, violet, violon* (sixteen, seven, purple, violin); *soleil, neige, treize, trois* (sun, snow, thirteen, three).

2. Divide the class into two teams. One pupil from each team comes to the board.

3. Display a set of words on the board and read them aloud. At your signal, the first pupil to point to the correct word – which doesn't belong to the list – wins a point. Those pupils return to their seats and are replaced by two others. Rub the words off the board.

4. Display four more words on the board and repeat the process. The team with the most points at the end of the session wins.

Useful phrases

Faites deux équipes.	Divide into two teams.
Venez au tableau.	Come to the board.
Montrez l'intrus.	Point to the odd one out.
Tu gagnes !	You win [to a single pupil]!

Comments

• You could add a speaking element to this game by asking pupils to say the words, pronouncing the key sound as accurately as possible. If their pronunciation is correct, they win an extra point for their team.

To increase the challenge, have two words that don't belong in each list of five or six words.

Bring in some writing by getting pupils to make up their own 'odd one out' sets to test the class.

13 Sound maze/*Le labyrinthe des sons*

Step by step

1. Decide which sound you want pupils to practise (see page 243). For example, for more advanced pupils, you may like to focus on the different common spellings of the sound 'in': *-in, -ein, -ain, -aim*. Prepare a grid with words that contain that sound and others that don't.

Classroom management	Whole class
Skill	Sounds
Aim	To make accurate sound–spelling links
Resources	Maze grid

For example:

			Sortie 1			Sortie 2	
	châtain	*malin*	*matin*	*train*	*pont*	*dessin*	*bain*
Départ	*chaton*	*malade*	*matou*	*tram*	*pain*	*dessus*	*lapin*	*Sortie 3*
	marron	*daim*	*vingt*	*son*	*plein*	*démon*	*cousin*
	marin	*dent*	*vilain*	*saint*	*plan*	*demain*	*faim*
				Sortie 4			

2. Display a copy of the maze on the board or whiteboard. Point to each word and read it aloud so pupils are aware of the pronunciation before they start the game.

3. Decide on a path through the maze, only reading out the words with the sound in focus. Starting from Depart, pupils can jump to any word in the next column. Pupils look at the maze and spot the words which you are reading. If they follow the route correctly, they should reach the correct exit. For example:

   T: *Marin, daim, vingt, train, pain, demain* (sailor, deer, twenty, train, bread, tomorrow). (Answer: Sortie 4.)

4. Check which exit pupils have reached. The class score one point if most pupils have reached the correct one; one point to you if more than half the class haven't.

Useful phrases		
	Écoutez les mots.	Listen to the words.
	Suivez les mots dans le labyrinthe.	Follow the words in the maze.
	À quelle sortie êtes-vous ?	Which exit did you reach?
	Bonne réponse !	Correct answer!
	Mauvaise réponse !	Wrong answer!

Comments

- Start reading a word on the left and work your way towards an exit on the right. You can't go backwards and the next word you say must be in the next column on the right.
- As an extension game, hand out a photocopy of the grid for pupils to play in pairs. They take turns at giving their partner a route.

 You can vary the level of challenge by having fewer or more columns in the maze.

Notes

14 Read my lips/*Paroles de muets*

Step by step

1. Decide which sounds pupils are going to practise (see page 243) and prepare a list with words containing those sounds.

2. Pupils work in pairs: hand a list to each pair. Pupils take turns selecting a word from the list and mouthing it to their partner, who tries to work out which word it is. If Pupil A mouths, for example, *bonbon* and Pupil B guesses correctly and says aloud *bonbon*, Pupil A gets a point. If Pupil B can't work out the word, Pupil A doesn't get a point.

Classroom management	Pair-work
Skill	Sounds
Aim	To read and produce sounds accurately
Resources	A list of words

Useful phrases

Choisissez un mot.   Choose a word.

Dites le mot silencieusement.   Mouth the word.

Regardez la bouche de votre partenaire.   Watch your partner's mouth.

Devinez le mot !   Guess the word!

Comments

• This game makes pupils aware of the importance of getting their mouths in the right shape to produce the sounds they want to produce, especially for vowel sounds.

 To increase the challenge, don't provide a list of words. Allow pupils to use any words they know containing a particular sound (if possible, the words should relate to the topic you're studying).

Notes

....

....

....

15 Sound omelette/*L'omelette de sons*

Step by step

1. Choose a phonetic point you would like pupils to practise, for example, the consonant sounds 'g' and 'j'.

2. Prepare your egg boxes. Write a word with one of the sounds you have chosen in each section of the egg box (or stick on a small label). For example: *gâteau, genou, géographie, girafe, gomme, goûter, guitare, jaune* (cake, knee, geography, giraffe, eraser, to taste, guitar, yellow).

Classroom management	Whole class
Skill	Sounds
Aim	To read and pronounce words accurately
Resources	One or several egg boxes (so you have 6, 10 or 12 sections) Beans or tokens

3. Divide the class into groups. Give each group an egg box and some beans.

4. The groups take turns placing a bean (or token) in the box. They close it and shake it. When they reopen the box, they read out the word in the section where the bean is. If they can say the word correctly, they win the bean.

5. Repeat the process several times. The group with the most beans wins.

Useful phrases

Mettez un haricot/un jeton dans la boîte.	Place a bean/token in the box.
Secouez !	Shake it!
Trouvez le haricot.	Find the bean.
Lisez le mot.	Read the word.

Comments

• Start saving egg boxes! If you only have one egg box, you can still play the game as a whole class, with the box circulating round the class.

Increase the challenge by increasing the number of beans. If several beans fall into the same section, pupils win all of them. If pupils cannot say all the words, they lose all their beans.

16 Scaredy cat!/*Gare au chat !*

Step by step

Classroom management	Whole class
Skill	Sounds
Aim	To read and pronounce words accurately
Resources	Non-transparent bag Cards or lolly sticks

1. Decide which sound you want pupils to practise (see page 243 for a list of sounds). For example, for more advanced pupils, you may like to focus on the different common spellings of the sound 'o': *-o, -ô, -au, -eau, -ot, -aux, -eaux.*

2. Write the words you want to practise on cards (or lolly sticks). On two or three cards (depending on the overall number of cards) write the word *chat !* (cat!). Make two sets with the same cards in each. Place each set in a non-transparent bag.

3. Divide the class into two teams, each sitting in a circle.

4. Pass the bag to the first pupil in each team. She takes out a card (or stick) and reads the word aloud. If she can pronounce it correctly, she can keep the card (or stick). If not, she must put it back in the bag. She then passes the bag to the next pupil in the team, and so on.

5. If she is not able to read the word correctly, she must put the card (or stick) back in the bag and pass it to the next person.

6. If a pupil pulls out a card that says *chat !*, the team loses all the cards they have already won and puts them all back in the bag. The game continues. The team with the most cards/sticks at the end of a given time is the winner.

Useful phrases

Tire une carte/un bâtonnet.	Pick a card/a lolly stick [to a single pupil].
Lis le mot.	Read the word [to a single pupil].
Attention à la prononciation !	Mind how you pronounce it!
Passe le sac à ton voisin/ta voisine.	Pass the bag to your neighbour [to a single pupil].
Remettez toutes vos cartes/ bâtonnets dans le sac.	Put all your cards/sticks back in the bag.

Comments

- This is based on the traditional English game of Scaredy cat. You could also play the game with each team drawing a scarecrow (using six sections). Whichever team has the most cards/sticks when they finish drawing the scarecrow wins.

To increase the challenge, work on several different sounds and mix cards from various sets.

Notes

....

....

....

....

....

....

....

....

....

....

....

....

....

....

17 Happy families/*Le jeu des sept familles*

Step by step

This game is based on the traditional game of Happy families. The aim is to collect all the cards belonging to one family. It is easily adapted to practise pronunciation.

Classroom management	Group work
Skill	Sounds
Aim	To read and produce sounds accurately
Resources	Home-made playing cards

1. Prepare the cards: for four groups, you will need four sets. Each set consists of seven families, each representing a different sound. For example: *la famille « on »* (the 'on' family, etc.), *la famille « en »*, *la famille « oi »*, *la famille « u »*, *la famille « ou »*, *la famille « in »*, *la famille « o »*.

   Each family has six (or four) cards with a different word using that sound written in large letters on the middle of each. The other words in the 'family' are written in smaller letters at the bottom of the card. For example, for 'oi', you could use: *une voiture* (a car), *un roi* (a king), *un poisson* (a fish), *une poire* (a pear), *un oiseau* (a bird) or *une étoile* (a star).

2. Divide the class into groups. Give each group a set of forty-two (or twenty-eight) cards, which they divide out randomly between the players.

3. The aim is to collect all the cards to make a complete family. The youngest pupil in each group starts by asking the person next to him for one particular card:

   P1: *Dans la famille « oi », je voudrais la voiture* (In the 'oi' family, I'd like the car).

   P2: *Voici la voiture.* (Here's the car.) [hands card over] or *Désolé(e)* (Sorry).

   It is then P2's turn to ask the next person:

   P2: *Dans la famille « on », je voudrais le melon.*

4. The winner in each team is the pupil who makes one (or more) complete family. The winning group is the first group to finish the game.

Mettez-vous en groupes.	Get into groups.
Distribuez toutes les cartes.	Deal out all the cards.
Demandez les cartes pour faire une famille.	Ask for the cards to make a family set.

Comments

- Instead of preparing the cards yourself, get pupils to make them! They prepare the cards as above. They could illustrate each word with a drawing.

This game is a great opportunity to get pupils using French with a real purpose – in order to play a game. Encourage them to use polite phrases such as *s'il te plaît* (please), *désolé(e)*, *je n'ai pas le/la/les …* (Sorry, I haven't got the …), *C'est à moi* (it's my turn), *c'est à toi* (it's your turn). Also, *J'ai une famille !* (I have a complete set!), *j'ai gagné !* (I've won!), etc.

Notes

18 Tongue-twisters/*Virelangues*

Step by step

1. Choose a tongue-twister (see the list on page 248) and write it on the board. Practise saying the tongue-twister with the whole class. Point out that pupils might find it easier to start at the end, repeating every two or three words several times before adding on the preceding bit. For example:

Classroom management	Whole class
Skill	Sounds
Aim	To read and produce sounds accurately
Resources	Tongue-twisters

L'ami Lili lit le livre au lit.

= au lit,

le livre au lit,

lit le livre au lit,

Lili lit le livre au lit,

L'ami Lili lit le livre au lit.

2. Divide the class into two teams. Everyone stands up. Recite the tongue-twister with the whole class first, slowly.
3. Pupils from Team A take turns saying the tongue-twister. When they get it right, they sit down. If they can't say it without tripping up, they remain standing.
4. Repeat the process with Team B.
5. Start another round with the pupils who are standing. The winning team is the team with most pupils sitting down at the end of the second round.

Useful phrases

Faites deux équipes.	Divide into two teams.
Lisez et répétez.	Read and repeat.
C'est bien ! Assieds-toi.	Well done! Sit down [to a single pupil].
Reste debout.	Stay standing [to a single pupil].

Comments

• Tongue-twisters are useful to practise pronunciation, especially if the sound does not exist in English or is pronounced differently. However, pupils can get frustrated if they are too hard or too long, so choose carefully!

• A variation is to have pupils take turns saying just one word of the tongue-twister each.

For example:

P1: *L'ami*

P2: *Lili*

P3: *lit*

P4: *le*

P5: *livre*

P6: *au*

P7: *lit.*

- See how many times you can get around the classroom. If you have a stopwatch, use it to see how fast the class can do it. Alternatively, divide the class into two groups and see which group does it the fastest.

 To increase the challenge, you could introduce an element of speed or repetition. Pupils must say the tongue-twister several times, as quickly as they can.

Notes

....

....

....

....

....

....

....

....

....

....

....

19 Test your strength/*Tour de force*

Step by step

1. Divide the class into two teams.

2. Draw two 'test-o-meters' on the board, one for each team. Choose a sound and write it at the top. For example, 'oi' or 'ou' or 'on'.

Classroom management	Whole class
Skill	Sounds
Aim	To write words with specific sounds
Resources	None

3. Two or three pupils from each team come to the board. They must write six words containing that sound along the test-o-meter. The rest of the team can help, but will have to send an envoy to the front of the class to whisper the word as they can't shout out words in case the other team hears them.

4. The first team to reach the top with six words spelled correctly wins.

5. Play again with a different sound and different pupils at the board.

 Useful phrases

Faites deux équipes.	Divide into two teams.
Écrivez des mots avec le son « X ».	Write words containing the sound '*X*'.
C'est correct.	It's correct.
Ce n'est pas correct.	It's not correct.

Comments

- A variation is to use a large sponge die to elicit words with different sounds: write six different sounds on sticky labels and fix them to each side of the die, for example, 'on', 'en', 'oi', 'in', 'ou', 'ai'.

- Alternatively, make a spinning wheel with a different sound on each segment.

 To increase the level of challenge, increase the number of words pupils have to either fill in or come up with to get to the top and win.

20 Little mouse/*Au lit, petite souris*

Step by step

The aim of the game is to fill in the board with words related to the topic and containing the sound in focus.

Classroom management	Whole class
Skill	Sounds
Aim	To write words with specific sounds
Resources	Board for game (see below) Bilingual dictionaries

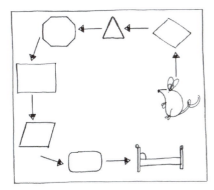

1. Divide the class into groups of four to six pupils. Give each group a board (as shown here; the board should be laminated, if you can) or ask them to draw one quickly on a sheet of paper.

2. Decide on a sound to practise (see page 243) and a topic (maybe the one you are working on or a previous topic for revision).

3. Pupils have to think of six words containing the chosen sound and write them down on the board so that the mouse can move along towards her bed.

4. Groups feed back to the class, starting with: *Avant d'aller au lit, la souris va* ... (Before going to bed, the mouse is going to ...)

   Avant d'aller au lit, la souris va manger ... (eat + food)

   Avant d'aller au lit, la souris va mettre ... (wear + clothes)

   Avant d'aller au lit, la souris va jouer/faire ... (play/do + sports, games), etc.

5. The winner is the group who has filled in the board correctly in the shortest time.

Useful phrases

Mettez-vous en groupes de 4–6.	Divide into groups of four to six.
Dessinez le parcours de la souris.	Draw the mouse's route.
Trouvez six mots avec le son « X ».	Find six words containing the sound 'X'.
Écrivez les mots sur le parcours.	Write the words on the board.

Comments

- For younger or less advanced pupils, provide labelled images of the items for them to use, or give the first and last letters of each word.

 More advanced pupils could use bilingual dictionaries to look for new words. This provides a good opportunity to explore new vocabulary and to work out how to pronounce unfamiliar words.

Appendix 1
French sounds

Vowel sounds	Letters	Examples
a	a/à/â	*ma, là, âne*
i	i/î/ï/y	*hiver, île, maïs, pyjama*
o	o/ô/au/eau	*rose, fauteuil, tableau*
e	e/eu/œu	• *cheval, bleu, œufs* (closed eu sound) • *fleur/œuf* (open eu sound)
é	é/ée/er/ez	*bébé, musée, aller, nez*
è	è/ë/ê/es/est/et/ai/ei	*mère, Noël, fête, les, (il) est, violet, clair, baleine*
u	u	*lune*
ou	ou/oo/ow	*rouge, cool, clown*
oi	oi	*noir*

Nasal sounds		
an	an/en/am/em	*orange, dent, jambe, décembre*
in	in/im/ain/aim/ein/ (i)en/(o)in/ (un)	*fin, timbre, main, faim, ceinture* *chien, loin* *(un, parfum)*
on	on/om	*marron, trompe*
ye	i/y/il/ill	*avion, yaourt, soleil, vanille*

Consonant sounds (with variations)		
j	j/g	*jeu, girafe*
z	s/z	*maison, zèbre*
s	s/ss/c/ç/x/t	*sapin, rousse, ciel, garçon, dix, attention*
f	f/ph	*feuille, pharmacie*
ch	ch/sh	*chat, shampooing*
k	c/k/qu/q/	*coq, kaki, quille, cinq*
g	g/gu	*gâteau, guitare*
ks	x	*taxi*
gz	x	*examen*
v	v/w	*voiture, wagon*

Appendix 2
French rhymes and tongue-twisters

Rhymes to practise specific sounds

« a »

Taratata	Taratata
le petit rat	the little rat
va chez Sacha	goes to the home of Sacha
le petit chat	the little cat
au Canada	in Canada

« i »

Lundi ... petit	Monday ... small
Mardi ... grandit	Tuesday ... grows
mercredi s'ennuie	Wednesday is bored
jeudi ... crie	Thursday ... shouts
vendredi ... rit	Friday ... laughs
samedi ... au lit	Saturday ... in bed
et dimanche	and Sunday
c'est fini !	it's over!

« o »

Je mets mon manteau	I put on my coat
Je mets mon chapeau	I put on my hat
Je fais du judo	I do judo
C'est rigolo.	It's funny.

« ou »

Debout, debout	Standing up
je suis un kangourou	I am a kangaroo
A genou, à genou,	Kneeling down
je suis un gros matou	I am a big tomcat

« oi »

Une oie	One goose
deux oies	Two geese
trois oies	Three geese
quatre oies	Four geese
cinq oies	Five geese
six oies	Six geese
c'est toi !	It's you!

« on »

Du poisson ?	Fish?
Non.	No.
Du jambon ?	Ham?
Non.	No.
Des champignons ?	Mushrooms?
Non.	No.
Du melon ?	Melon?
Non.	No.
Alors quoi donc ?	So what, then?
Des cornichons.	Gherkins.
Ah bon !	Oh, good!

« in »

Un lapin	One rabbit,
deux lapins,	Two rabbits,
trois lapins	Three rabits,
quatre lapins,	Four rabbits,
cinq lapins	Five rabbits,
dans mon jardin !	In my garden!

« u »

Loup, y es-tu ?	Wolf, are you there?
M'entends-tu ?	Can you hear me?
Que fais-tu ?	What are you doing?

« a » et « oi »

Le rat se moque du chat,	The rat makes fun of the cat,
Le chat se moque du rat,	The cat makes fun of the rat,
Tu te moques de moi,	You're making fun of me
Et qui se moque de toi ?	And who is making fun of you?
C'est moi !	It's me!

« k »
Un petit kiwi
Tout rikiki
En bikini
A mis K-O
Un kangourou
De cent kilos
En kimono.

A little kiwi bird
all rickety
wearing a bikini
has knocked out
a kangaroo
weighing a hundred kilos
wearing a kimono.

Mixed sounds
Voici ma main
Elle a cinq doigts
En voici deux
en voici trois

Here is my hand
It has five fingers
Here are two
Here are three

Il fait chaud, chaud, chaud,
il fait froid, froid, froid,
il fait chaud, il fait froid
chez toi !

It is hot, hot, hot
It is cold, cold, cold,
It is hot, it is cold,
At your house!

Am stram gram
Pic et pic et colégram
Bour et bour et ratatam
Am stram gram

Eenie Meenie
Peak and peak and colegram
Bour and bour and ratatam
Eenie Meenie

Un et un, deux
une poulette sans queue
deux et deux, quatre
une poulette sans pattes
quatre et quatre, huit
la poulette est cuite

One and one, two,
A chick without a tail,
Two and two, four,
A chick without legs,
Four and four, eight,
The chick is cooked!

Tongue-twisters/*Les virelangues*

Sounds	Tongue-twister
'i'	*L'ami Lili lit le livre au lit.* Our friend Lili reads a book in bed.
	Six slips chics. Six chic pants.
'a'/'i'	*Lila à Lilles et Lola au Lilas.* Lila in Lilles and Lola in Lilas.
'è'	*Le ver vert va vers le verre vert.* The green worm goes towards the green glass.
	Seize chaises sèchent. Sixteen chairs are drying.
	Mon père est maire. My father is the mayor.
'en'	*Ta tante t'attend dans ta tente.* Your aunt is waiting for you in your tent.
'on'	*Mon tonton tond ton tonton.* My uncle is shaving your uncle.
	Onze oncles, onze ongles, on jongle. Eleven uncles, eleven nails, we're juggling.
'ou'	*Douze douches douces.* Twelve gentle showers.
	La roue rouge roule. The red wheel is turning.
'oi'	*Trois loirs noirs dans la baignoire.* Three black dormice in the bathtub.
'ui'	*Huit truites cuites.* Eight cooked trouts.
'in'/'en'	*Des pains blancs, des bancs peints, des bains pleins.* White bread, painted benches, full bathtubs.
'im'/'en'/'on'	*Un dindon sans dents et un daim sans dédain.* A toothless (male) turkey and a deer without scorn.
'ss'/'ch'	*Six chiens chassent six chats.* Six dogs are chasing six cats.
	Six saucisses sèches. Six dry sausages.
	La mouche rousse touche la mousse. The red fly touches the moss.
	La chemise du chimiste sèche. The chemist's shirt is drying.
'r'	*Trois gros rats gris dans trois grands trous.* Three big grey rats in three big holes.
	Trop tard pour le tram trente-trois. Too late for the thirty-three tram.
'j'	*Angèle et Gilles gèlent en gilet.* Angèle and Gilles are freezing in their cardigans.
'k'/'ch'	*Le coq se choque et se chicane.* The cockerel is shocked and quibbles a lot.

Appendix 3
Quick and easy ways to turn a language activity into a competitive game

Adding a competitive element can make the most routine language activity into a motivating challenge! Imagine you want to ask comprehension questions about a text or new topic vocabulary. Why not try one of the following to make this more exciting?

Formula 1 racing

Draw a racetrack on the board. Divide the class into two teams. Each team has a different coloured racing car, which can be tacked to the board. Ask your comprehension questions. Each time a pupil gives a correct answer, their team is allowed to move their car forward one square. The first team to get to the end of the track wins.

Variations: Walking the plank, Hopscotch grids, Snakes and Ladders board, Blockbusters grid

Noughts and crosses

Draw a grid on the board. Divide the class into two teams. Ask your comprehension questions. Each time a pupil gives a correct answer their team can place their symbol in the grid. The winning team is the first to make a row of three.

Basketball

Take two or three wastepaper baskets. Fix a number on each to show its points value, e.g. 5, 10, 20. Every time a pupil answers a question correctly, she earns a turn to throw a ping-pong ball (or a ball made from a scrunched-up piece of paper) into a bin and win the corresponding number of points. The first team to 100 points wins. For a quicker version, set a lower winning total.

Cross the river

You need a large open space to play. Take some old newspapers and give two pages to each pupil. They line up at one side of the room. The aim is to cross to the other side, using the newspaper as stepping stones. Ask the first question. Anyone who gets it right can lay down their first sheet of paper and stand on it. Ask your second question. Anyone who is right lays their second piece of paper down in front, moves onto it and then picks up the first piece. Anyone who does not have the right answer does not move forward. The game continues until someone reaches the other side.

Beat the clock

Write your questions on the board before the class arrives. How quickly can pupils answer them all? Deduct 10 seconds for a wrong answer. The class could compete against each other in teams, or as a whole class against their previous personal best.

Joker cards

Make some joker cards. Ask individual pupils your comprehension questions. They win a point per correct answer. If a pupil can't answer or gets the answer wrong, he can ask you for a joker card. This allows him to nominate another pupil to help him. If the pupil nominated gives a correct answer, he gets the joker card and an additional point and the first pupil can carry on playing. If the nominated pupil can't answer or gives a wrong answer, the first pupil loses a turn.

Jigsaw

Divide the class into two teams and give each one the picture from a child's jigsaw puzzle (ideally one with not too many pieces). Each time a pupil answers a question correctly, she wins a piece of their jigsaw puzzle. The winning team is the one that completes their jigsaw first.

Offer a reward

- Write the winner's name inside an outline crown drawn on the board – they are the King or Queen for the day.
- Offer an incentive for the class if everyone (or, with less able groups, maybe if more than 80 per cent of the class) completes the task accurately. The actual incentive will depend on your group and your circumstances; ideas could include their choice of a song to sing at the end of the lesson, a sweet, house points, etc.